Love Songs of Early China

Geoffrey Sampson

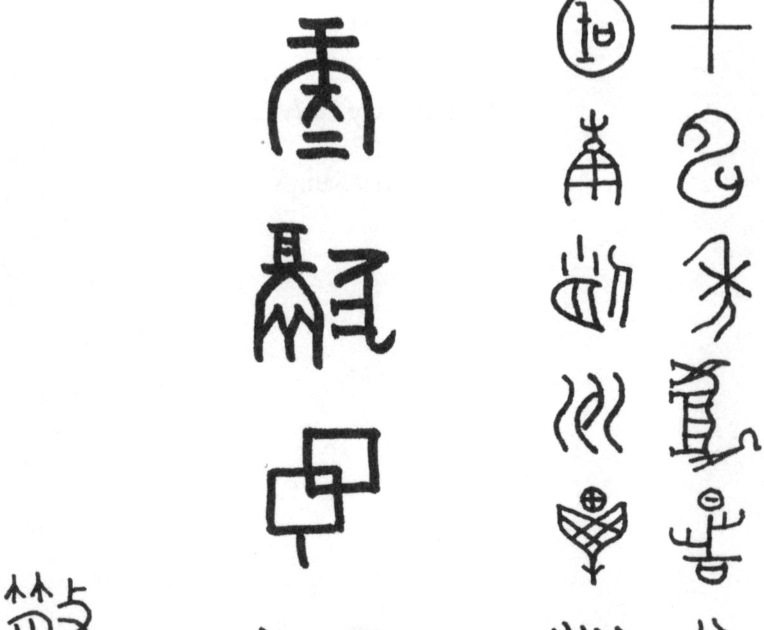

LOVE SONGS
OF EARLY CHINA

GEOFFREY SAMPSON

SHAUN TYAS
DONINGTON
2006

Typeset, designed and published by

SHAUN TYAS
1 High Street
Donington
Lincolnshire
PE11 4TA

ISBN
1 900289 75 X

Printed and bound by Woolnoughs of Irthlingborough

CONTENTS

CONTENTS

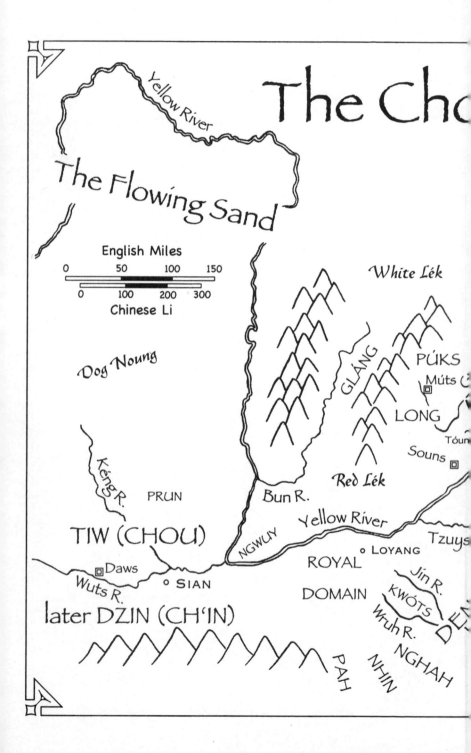

The Cho

Yellow River

The Flowing Sand

English Miles

| 0 | 50 | 100 | 150 |

| 0 | 100 | 200 | 300 |

Chinese Li

White Lék

Dog Noung

PÚKS

Múts

GLÁNG

LONG

Kéng R.

Tóun

Souns

PRUN

Red Lék

Bun R.

TIW (CHOU)

Daws

NGWUY

Yellow River

Tzuys

LOYANG

ROYAL

SIAN

Wuts R.

DOMAIN

Jin R.

KWÓTS

D

later DZIN (CH'IN)

Wruh R.

NGHAH

PAH

NHIN

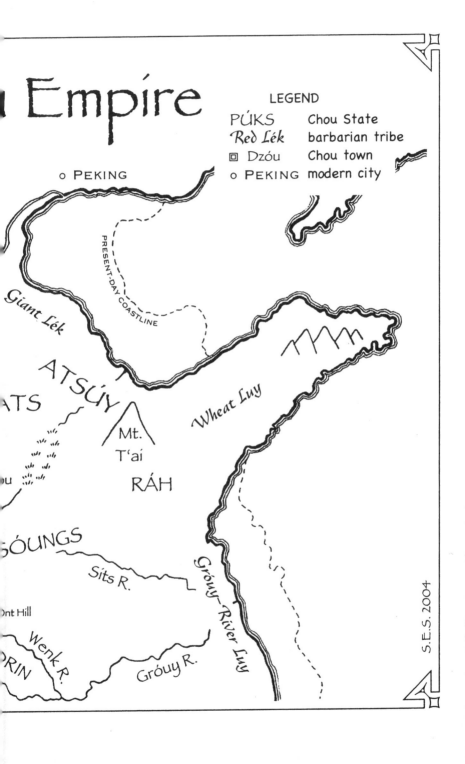

Empire

o PEKING

PRESENT-DAY COASTLINE

Giant Lék

ATSÚY

ATS

Mt.
T'ai

RÁH

Wheat *Luy*

SÓUNGS

Sits R.

ou

Ont Hill

Wenk R.

RIN

Gróuy R.

Gróuy River *Luy*

S.E.S. 2004

INTRODUCTION

Voices from a distant past

The songs or poems in this book are among the earliest literary works to have been written down anywhere in the world. They offer a rare window into the minds of individuals in a distant country, China, almost three thousand years ago.

Because Old Chinese was an unusually simple language in terms of structure, the window is unusually transparent. The book translates the poems into straightforward English prose, and on facing pages it uses our alphabet to show them as they sounded in the original Old Chinese. Anyone who cares to read the poems aloud can hear the rhymes and rhythms heard by the original poets; it is easy to look up the words of the short lines in the glossary provided and see how the lines mean what the English says they mean. This is one of the few cases – perhaps the only case – where we can readily understand people speaking to us, in their own voices, across millennia.

The poems are a selection from the book whose name in modern Mandarin Chinese is *Shih*, or more fully *Shih Ching* – the title has been translated into English variously as *Book of Odes*, *Classic of Songs*, or similar phrases. This is an anthology, which was traditionally said to have been compiled by Confucius (551–479 B.C.). That is highly doubtful; but whether it is true or not, the songs themselves are certainly older: they are believed to date to different periods from the tenth to seventh centuries.

Some of the anthology items would more naturally be called "poems" in English, while others we would be more likely to see as "songs", for instance songs to accompany physical work. To insist on a distinction between these terms would be to impose European literary categories on a culture to which they were foreign. Chinese has no single word covering the various things that we call "poetry"; conversely, the word *shih* in the anthology title (in Old Chinese it was pronounced *stu*) covers all the different kinds of item it contains. Consequently I treat the English terms "poem" and "song" as interchangeable here; and I shall refer to the anthology by its Old Chinese title, *Stu*.

From the 305 songs in the *Stu* I have selected ones which have a theme of love, interpreted widely. Not all such poems are included. Some items which would come under the heading of love are omitted because they are very similar to items which have been chosen. (When folk-songs are transmitted by word of mouth, it is no surprise to find variants developing which are partly the same and partly divergent.) Others have been omitted as too banal to interest a present-day audience – perhaps they were songs for which the music mattered more than the lyrics. (I have included one such, "Within the Gate-Screen", in order to allow readers to decide for themselves whether I was justified in leaving out others.) But the 58 poems presented in this volume represent the majority of *Stu* poems related to love. Unusually for ancient literature, many (indeed, most) are worded from the woman's point of view.

Older roots than ours

It is worth taking a moment to reflect on how very old these poems are, in terms of history with which most of us are more familiar. The poems selected for this book are in fact among the latest in the *Stu*, dating from the decades leading up to and following 700 B.C. (The earlier *Stu* songs are ritual hymns, more impersonal and consequently less interesting to the present-day reader.) The poems included here go back "only" 27 centuries or so; but that is a long time.

England was not yet England in 700 B.C.: it would be more than a thousand years before the Angles and Saxons came to Britain. For that matter, Britain was probably not yet Britain; it is unclear when the Celts or "Ancient Britons" arrived, but the scholarly consensus seems to place it rather later than the latest *Stu* poems. We know little about the people who lived in Britain before the Celts; they appear to have been largely nomadic herdsmen. We have no idea what language or languages they spoke, or whether these were related to any languages known to recorded history – they certainly had no idea of writing. The classical civilizations of Europe were only beginning to get off the ground. This was the time when the Greeks first learnt to use the alphabet; the legendary date of the foundation of Rome by Romulus and Remus was 753 B.C.

In China, matters were different. The Chinese led settled lives; many of them lived in walled towns. Those who could afford it got about in carriages. Their culture was already moderately sophisticated, politically, technically, and artistically. They spoke an earlier version of the language which their descendants in the same territory speak today: Chinese. And we know these things because they have told us.

2

For centuries before the time of these poems, Chinese was already a written language. The script used to write Chinese at that period looks superficially unlike modern Chinese writing – later changes in writing materials caused curves to give way to straight lines and angles, leading to a more abstractly stylized appearance; but a brief examination quickly reveals how one is a direct evolution from the other.

While the *Stu* is among the world's oldest literary productions, it is of course far from being the oldest of all. The poetry of Sumer (in what is now Iraq), for instance the epic tales of Gilgamesh, date to the third millennium B.C. However, the Sumerians and their language had vanished from the historical record a thousand years before the time of these Chinese love songs. China is the oldest civilization in the world which continues to flourish in essentially unbroken continuity today.

Emperor and States

Although Chinese civilization reaches back more than three thousand years, it did not always occupy the whole territory now called "China". It began in the middle reaches of the Yellow River and its tributaries; in various directions from that area, the early Chinese were surrounded by "barbarians" – non-Chinese-speaking tribal societies which were less culturally advanced, and probably somewhat distinct racially.

The period of the *Stu* songs is known in Chinese history as the Chou dynasty. The name "Chou" (pronounced roughly like English Joe) was originally the name of a western section of the Chinese cultural area, around present-day Sian. Some time in the eleventh century (perhaps in 1045 B.C., but the exact date is uncertain) a Chou leader took control of the entire Chinese area and divided it into States, which he gave to various relatives and allies to rule under his and his successors' overall authority. By this time, the Chinese had spread eastwards across the North China plain, as far as the sea in some areas (though other coastal areas were still tribal).

As the centuries passed, successive Chou emperors' relationship to the States gradually faded from real political control into a vaguer religious authority over what became effectively independent kingdoms. At the period represented by our love songs, this loss of political strength had recently been underlined, when rebel States in alliance with barbarians attacked the original Chou capital and killed the emperor. After 771 B.C., later Chou emperors actually ruled only a small "royal domain" around present-day Loyang, downstream from their original homeland.

3

Some things that we think of as central to Chinese life were not yet part of it. Rice, if known at all, was not a significant crop; it will not grow in the arid environment where the Chinese originated. The traditional staple food was millet – though wheat had been introduced by the beginning of the Chou dynasty, and is often mentioned in these poems. (One coastal tribe was called the "Wheat Luy", suggesting that when the Chinese first encountered them this diet was distinctive.) Not that the Chinese were fussy about their diet – living in fairly unfriendly terrain, with early technology, they needed to eat whatever was edible. To learn about some of the food crops mentioned in these poems, I visited websites which advise modern Man on wilderness survival.

The emperor's power was weakening, but the Chinese cultural area continued to expand – particularly southwards, where there were few natural barriers. Chinese States conquered adjacent tribes and gradually absorbed them, and barbarian rulers adopted cultural and political practices of their powerful neighbours voluntarily. By the time of our poems, China extended down to the Yangtze River; after a further 500 years, Chinese rule would spread as far as the south coast in the Hong Kong area. The same pattern, of Chinese inhabiting a heartland while non-Chinese maintained some cultural and ethnic distinctiveness under Chinese rule in peripheral areas, has continued on a wider geographical scale to this day.

A fluid geography

Each poem in this collection is associated with a specific State or town, and many of them mention particular places (though in one or two cases the places named in a poem do not match the State to which the poem is traditionally ascribed). The map on pp. viii–ix is included to lend concrete reality to the landscape of the poems,[1] and each poem is followed by the name of the place where it originated. But do not look for these names in a modern atlas: you will not find them.

The map shows rough locations for each place mentioned; but it would be meaningless to plot exact boundaries of the States. Some of them were large territories, others were just one town and the countryside immediately surrounding it. As the decades passed, one State would expand its territory at the expense of a neighbour; a powerful State might swallow up a weak one entirely, or new States might be carved out of an existing State's territory. There may well have been no single year in which every State named on the map existed as a separate entity. And all of the States were swept away in the third century B.C., when Ch'in (which had moved in from the far

---

[1] I thank Sophia Sampson for drawing the map.

West to occupy the land vacated by Chou) conquered each of the other States and founded a unitary Chinese empire. (Our name "China" derives from Ch'in.) Even if a modern Chinese province coincides in territory with a Chou-dynasty State, it will have a different name.

In Europe, Athens and Rome are modern capitals on ancient sites, and classical buildings can still be seen there; but Chinese towns have traditionally been more temporary affairs. Chinese buildings were not designed to be everlasting. There were no cathedrals. A "palace" was not an imposing stone building visible to any passer-by; it was a walled park or compound, containing various wooden halls which were certainly more spacious and better-appointed than the residences of subjects, but were not built on a monumental scale. (There was little need for them to impress, because only the élite who had business in the palace would ever see them.) We know where some towns mentioned in the poems were, but they do not coincide with modern cities.

Even the central geographical feature of the original Chinese heartland, the Yellow River, shares this character of impermanence. The Yellow River is very different from any river of Europe. It is called Yellow because of the heavy burden of loess soil its waters carry, on their way southwards from the desert which we call the Gobi and in Old Chinese was called *Rou Sháy*, "the Flowing Sands". As the river reaches the plains, the soil settles out so that the bed of the river is constantly rising, and the banks have to be built up artificially to contain it. (At present, near what was the Chou royal domain, the river bed is more than fifty feet higher than the surrounding land.) Sooner or later, in times of storm and high water, the river has repeatedly broken out, destroying many livelihoods and finding some new way to the sea.

Currently, the mouth of the river is on the Gulf of Pohai. Only 150 years ago it was three hundred miles further south, on the other side of the hilly Shantung peninsula. There have been times in Chinese history when the Yellow River was a tributary of the Yangtze, far to the south. At the time of these poems, conversely, it formed a vast delta whose main branch reached the sea well to the north of its present-day course, somewhere near the site of modern Peking. (A secondary branch, called the Tzúys, was then one of the great rivers of China; it no longer exists.) The coastline itself has shifted: the North China plain is the product of these continuing river-borne deposits, and in the Chou dynasty the coast ran a hundred miles or more inland from its present position.

The historical continuity of China is a continuity of culture. Physically, the country is a palimpsest on which Nature and successive dynasties have written, erased, and rewritten, again and again.

Why revive the original pronunciation?

At first sight, presenting these songs in their original pronunciation might seem to be an empty exercise in scholarly antiquarianism. In fact, it is the only way to bring them to life for a present-day audience.

Old Chinese is so different from any language of Europe that attempts to "translate" the *Stu* poems into one of our poetic forms can at best yield new, Western poems, inspired by but only very distantly connected to the Chinese originals. Such attempts have been made, and they can be enjoyable to read – but one is not reading the *Stu*.

A Chinese-speaker will normally approach the *Stu* songs by giving the words their modern Chinese pronunciation – just as we act Shakespeare in modern English, even though the experts know full well that many of his words sounded different in the sixteenth century. With Shakespeare it would be silly to do otherwise: nothing is lost by using the sounds which are familiar to modern audiences. But so much has changed in Chinese, over the far longer period since the *Stu* songs were composed, that someone who approaches them in terms of modern Chinese pronunciation has little opportunity to appreciate them as anything more than obscure academic curiosities.

Often, the "sound-music" of the *Stu* wording drives the meaning as much as the other way round – just as it does in our own folk-songs. When the anonymous author of "Tavern in the Town" sings:

> I'll hang my harp on a weeping willow-tree
> And may the world go well with thee

we surely do not think to question whether a weeping-willow would really be a practical thing to lodge a harp on. That would take the song at quite the wrong level. But we can take the song at its own level because we can feel the rhythm, we can hear "thee" rhyming with "tree", and so forth. The word-music of the *Stu* songs is very simple (as one might expect, with such early poetry), but in modern Chinese these simple sound-effects have wholly evaporated through almost three thousand years of language evolution.

Words which rhymed in the first millennium B.C. commonly do not rhyme in modern Mandarin Chinese. What is more, even where words do still rhyme, the impact of a rhyme is different: Mandarin has much less variety of sound patterns than Old Chinese had, so rhymes are far more common. The *Stu* makes heavy use of expressive two-syllable words, like *trent-tront*, to toss and turn, or *hóuy-lóuy*, worn out. These "rhymers and chimers" were a characteristic feature of Old Chinese vocabulary, and they are frequent in some East Asian languages, such as Vietnamese, today; but, as it happens, they have almost entirely vanished from Mandarin.

Consequently, someone who approaches the *Stu* through the medium of modern Chinese is in a similar position to a person who reads the wording of "There is a Tavern in the Town" without knowing which syllables are stressed, or which words rhyme: that really would be a dry academic exercise. To grasp what the *Stu* songs were, for their original singers, one needs to hear the sounds which they heard. And for a Western reader, with no prior assumptions in favour of modern Chinese pronunciation, that is not a challenging task. The song lines are very short (commonly just four syllables), making it easy to take in the sounds from the printed page.

Presenting the *Stu* poems in Old Chinese not only reveals sound-effects that would otherwise be lost, but also avoids special difficulties which modern Chinese poses for a Western audience. Many readers will know that Chinese is a "tone language": words are distinguished not only by distinctive vowels and consonants but also by distinctive patterns of pitch. These tones have been crucial to Chinese poetic art. The golden age of Chinese poetry was that of the T'ang and Sung dynasties, from the seventh to eleventh centuries of the Christian era: the poetry of that period depended on metrical rules about alternating tones, as European poetic metre depends on rules for alternating stressed and unstressed syllables. But tones are inaudible to untrained Western ears. And the vowels and consonants of modern Mandarin often sound undistinctive and confusing to us.

The Old Chinese of the *Stu*, although it is ancestral to T'ang-dynasty Chinese and to modern Mandarin, sounded very different from either of them. Old Chinese was not a tone language – the tones developed later. And the patterns of vowels and consonants in Old Chinese are more comparable to those we are accustomed to in European languages. Poetic effects in the *Stu* depend on sound features which are familiar in Western poetry. We can hear them without difficulty.

Over and above these considerations, there is surely a kind of magic about hearing human beings reveal their hearts, in the very sounds which they uttered so unimaginably long ago.

Names
One decision I had to make in compiling this book was how to spell proper names. Normally, even long-obsolete names are spelled in terms

of their modern Mandarin pronunciation. The modern Chinese name for the Gobi desert is essentially the same as our name; but if anyone had occasion to refer to the ancient name "Flowing Sands", they would write it as Mandarin *Liu Sha*, not Old Chinese *Rou Sháy*. The river Tzúys vanished long ago, but someone who mentioned it today would normally call it the Chi – that is the Mandarin syllable which "Tzúys" has turned into after many centuries of sound-changes.

Within the Chinese versions of the poems, I must of course print names in their Old Chinese pronunciation, along with all the other words. Since the names in the poems are almost without exception names that have lost any relevance in a present-day context, it would be unnecessarily confusing to spell them one way in the Chinese texts and a quite different way in the English translations. The names in the poems are written in Old Chinese, not just on the Chinese pages but in the translations and on the map.

There are just two names in the poems which the general reader might well encounter elsewhere, namely the successive dynasty names Chou and Ch'in, which in Old Chinese were *Tiw* and *Dzin*. In these cases I have compromised, using the modern forms within the English translations.

Chinese names not belonging to the Chou period which happen to be mentioned in this Introduction or elsewhere in the book are written in their Mandarin form, as traditionally represented within English-language writing.[1]

Cutting through complexities

Some readers may be surprised to hear that the language of these poems is easily accessible to a modern Western audience. Things Chinese often have a reputation for impenetrable complexity.

One reason for that reputation is the intricate Chinese script – but in this book it is not used. The Chinese pages use our alphabet to display the words of the poems in Old Chinese pronunciation.

In recent centuries, because of divergence of dialects and for other reasons, the phonetic identity of Chinese words has become so confusing, and the written characters have become so crucial a key to word-identities, that a Chinese can easily feel that the essence of his

---

[1] The Chinese have devised an alternative system for alphabetizing Mandarin, and this has been widely adopted in the West since the 1970s; in this new system the names Chou and Ch'in, for instance, become "Zhou" and "Qin". But in a literary context the traditional romanization system used in the present book still seems better-established than this newer alternative.

language lies in its traditional written form: Chinese without Chinese script is not Chinese. But at the period of these poems, the factors that make for phonetic confusion had not yet emerged. An alphabetic script is as suitable for Old Chinese as for a European language. Chinese script, in the Chou dynasty, was merely a tool created for recording the words of speech: no less and no more. This book uses an alternative tool which happens to be easier for Western readers to handle. In the case of work songs, it is quite unlikely that their Chou-dynasty singers would have been literate themselves – so it would be hard to argue that an appreciation of the songs depends crucially on seeing the Chinese script.

Just the titles of the selected poems are shown in this book, for the sake of decoration, in the relatively naturalistic version of Chinese script that was current at the period.[1]

There are other reasons, though, why readers might expect these poems to be more obscure than they are. People in the English-speaking world who know anything of Chinese poetry are most likely to have encountered the T'ang and Sung lyric poets – writers such as Li Po or Po Chü-i. That literature is subtle and beautiful, for those who can understand it, but understanding it is often difficult. China under the T'ang had been a mighty and complex civilization for a very long time. (The T'ang capital was easily the most populous and probably the most technologically advanced city anywhere in the world; the West only caught up much later, through our Industrial Revolution.) Poets and their audiences took for granted a large shared stock of historical and literary knowledge, and writers drew on this freely to achieve their own literary effects. As a result, many of these effects are lost on us, and have to be explained via clumsy footnotes.

Chou-dynasty China by contrast was a young civilization that had not had time to build up a resource of cultural references. The poems in this book speak directly to us about human beings and the natural world. Their wording perhaps sometimes borders on the naïve – certainly, this is not love poetry with the intellectual subtlety of a Shakespeare or a Donne. But the directness makes it clear; and how

---

[1] It is the difference between these early script-forms, scratched on bone, and the modern brush-and-ink script which evolved later, that enables me to offer examples of the former in the poem titles and on the dedication page. Calligraphy is a universal accomplishment among educated Chinese and ranks as their highest-valued art; for a Westerner to display his childish hand publicly would be shameful. But no-one now writes the so-called "oracle bone" script, so my scrawls are perhaps as acceptable as another's might be.

many opportunities do we have to see directly into the hearts of men and women who lived almost three millennia ago, naïve or not?

Another factor making the *Stu* appear less accessible than it really is has been the heavy apparatus of commentary and interpretation that has accrued round it. As an early literary monument of the world's oldest and most populous civilization, the *Stu* has been studied intensively for thousands of years. Some commentators have done very useful work (which my translations draw on) in clarifying obsolete vocabulary, but it must be said that others have created unnecessary obscurities.

As China grew richer and more powerful, it became a somewhat pompous society, which lost sight of the simplicity of life in the Chou era. To many commentators, it was evidently inconceivable that a great classic work could have dealt with mere everyday relationships between men and women; they reinterpreted the poems as allegorical descriptions of high political events.

The song "The North Wind" tells of a woman who is seeking to join a man: according to one tradition of commentary, she was the queen of a conquered State requesting asylum with a noble ally. But, if one reads the words for their plain meaning, the song seems to be about a girl in dire straits trying to sell her body in exchange for shelter on a winter night – and I take it that is indeed what was intended. Again, commentators on "The Red Pipe" wondered how a respectable girl could be meeting a man in public, unchaperoned. Under later dynasties, she might not have been able to; but a complex social machinery for keeping women secluded depends on a society having sufficient resources to maintain the machinery, and to forgo the women's potential economic contributions. Chou society was simpler and poorer; on the evidence of these poems, relationships between unmarried men and girls were relaxed, more comparable to what we have known in the West in recent times than to later Chinese norms. We know that, outside the ranks of the aristocracy, it was not usual for a girl to marry before she was pregnant.

Western as well as Chinese commentators have debated whether the poems should be seen as folk songs composed by anonymous members of the common people, or as products of the literate élite. The answer may well be different for different poems, but it is also likely that in some respects social differences under the Chou were narrower than they later became. Emmanuel Le Roy Ladurie has commented about fourteenth-century society in the French Pyrenees that "there was no absolute distinction between artisan and peasant ... or even between artisan and noble. In this part of the world, everybody worked with his hands". Chou China was certainly no egalitarian democracy; at the time of our poems, it was just beginning to evolve from a feudal society where the only intermediate status between peasant labourers and hereditary nobility was the class of administrators employed by the latter, into a society where a man of the people who had business talent could rise through his own efforts. Nevertheless, even noble birth may not have removed its possessors from the sphere of physical work so entirely as gentlemanly status was to do under later dynasties.

The simplicity of the Old Chinese language

Paradoxically, the language of the *Stu* is far more accessible to us than that of the early literary monuments of Europe. The Chinese anthology is broadly comparable in age to the Homeric epics, the *Iliad* and *Odyssey* (which were composed orally well before they were first written down). But Greek and Latin literature can be understood in the original only by the few who are willing to spend years mastering the very complex grammar of the classical European languages.

Chinese, and particularly Old Chinese, could not be more different. Essentially, it is a language without grammar. Words are invariant: there are no distinctions of singular versus plural nouns, or variations of tense or mood in verbs. No words are irregular, because there is nothing to be regular or otherwise. A line of poetry is simply a sequence of lumps of meaning, with only their order to show the logical relationships among them. Furthermore, the word-order is essentially similar to English. The subject, if it appears at all, precedes the verb, and the object normally follows. Adjectives come before nouns, rather than after as in French ("white house" versus *maison blanche*). Someone who reads a line of Old Chinese and looks its words up in the glossary is fully equipped to appreciate its meaning.

There are features of the language that contrast with what we are used to. Probably the most important is that subjects are optional and commonly do not appear. In written English, every statement must have a subject, though if the doer of the action is obvious from the context then this can be just a short pronoun – he, she, you, or I, for instance. In Chinese, if a writer does not want to specify the doer of the action, it is left out. Colloquially, in English we say things like "Went to the Palace yesterday" (usually meaning "I went ..."). In Chinese this kind of sequence is normal even in formal writing, and it might stand for "I went ...", or "she went ...", or "they went ...", or other possibilities.

One consequence is that it can be hard to know whether to translate a poem into the first or third person – is the poet describing his own life, or someone else's? To a Chinese reader, that might seem a pointless question: the poem is what it is, it makes some things explicit and leaves others vague. It has often been said that in this respect Chinese poetry is akin to Chinese landscape painting. In a European painting, every inch is covered with paint; but a Chinese painter will place a mountain here, a tree there, a stream over there, and leave the blanks for the viewer to fill in from imagination.

William Empson argued in *Seven Types of Ambiguity* that ambiguity is of the essence of all poetry.[1] Even if that is true, though, ambiguity is certainly more salient in Chinese poetry than in any European language. Not just the lack of subjects, but the fewness of grammatical devices of any sort, mean that there is far more room than we are used to for the reader to interpret a line one way or another way. The logical explicitness of European languages forces a translator to choose one reading and impose it, but alternative readings will often be fully defensible. Ambiguity and grammatical simplicity are two sides of one coin: if Old Chinese were more logically precise, it would be less accessible to us than it is.

Apart from the optionality of subjects, Old Chinese naturally does have a few other special linguistic wrinkles. If the object is a pronoun, it sometimes precedes the verb, as in French (*je le vois*, rather than "I see him"). There is no verb "to be": a noun is equated to another noun by suffixing the word *lay* ("John is the king" would be "John king *lay*"), but for "John is wise" one would normally just say the equivalent of "John wise". If a descriptive predicate is not abstract, like wisdom, but relatively tangible and physical, the word for it is commonly doubled. For instance, *tzáng* and *phóts* are two of many Old Chinese words meaning "luxuriant, thickly-growing": in "The Poplar by the East Gate", the idea "its leaves are thick" is expressed in the first verse as *gu lap tzáng-tzáng*, and in the second verse as *gu lap phóts-phóts*. (In the glossary, words are often listed singly even if they are doubled in the poems: *phóts* rather than *phóts-phóts*, and so on.) With a two-syllable word, each syllable is doubled separately: *oy-láy* "submissive, obedient" becomes *oy-oy-láy-láy*.

But these are very minor hurdles indeed to the task of grasping how Old Chinese words combine together to express thoughts. They do not compare with the problem of mastering verb endings even in a modern European language, let alone a classical language.

[1] Publication details for books and articles consulted in producing the present volume are listed on pp. 151–2.

No common origin

The one respect in which European languages are easier for us is that, normally, quite a number of their words turn out to be recognizably similar to their English equivalents. European languages share a common origin, and they have borrowed vocabulary from one another heavily. Old Chinese is an entirely separate language; its speakers had no contacts with speakers of the Indo-European family of languages to which English belongs. So, naturally, every single word, whether a rare word or a frequent word, is totally unrelated to its English equivalent. Someone who approaches this literature unaided has a great deal of dictionary work to do.

But, for readers of the present book, that work is already done. The vocabulary used in this selection of poems is not large, and all words used (and only those words) are conveniently listed in the glossary.

Strictly, I should add, it may be an overstatement to say that speakers of Old Chinese had never had any cultural contacts at all with Indo-European speakers. We know nowadays that one group of Indo-Europeans, the Tocharians (now long extinct), were living in what is now Sinkiang, north of Tibet, at least as early as the Old Chinese period. (A very readable book on the Tocharians is by Elizabeth Wayland Barber, *The Mummies of Ürümchi*.) There are tantalizing suggestions that some words may have been exchanged between the respective languages. For instance, the word for honey was *mit* in both Old Chinese and the "Tocharian B" language, and this is claimed not to be a coincidence: Chinese is said to have borrowed the Tocharian word. (If so, the Chinese for "honey" would ultimately stem from the same root as English "mead".) But cases like this, though fascinating, are so marginal that for practical purposes the general point stands.

How to pronounce Old Chinese

The spelling system I use for Old Chinese should not be difficult for an English-speaking reader to grasp. Most consonants have their expected values; *g* always has the hard sound of English get, not the soft sound of gem.

The letter *h* is used in several different ways. At the beginning of a syllable, *h* represents the sound in Scottish *loch* or Yiddish *chutzpah*. The combinations *ph*, *th*, *kh* represent a p, t, or k followed by a puff of breath. (Old Chinese had no sounds akin to those of English have, phone, thing.) After consonants like *l* or *m*, an *h* represents a "voiceless" version of those consonants, for instance *lh* is the Welsh "ll" in a name like Llangollen. The combinations *sh*, *ch*, *zh* stand for sounds akin to those in English shush, church, measure, but these Old Chinese sounds (and also that written *j*) were what is called "retroflex", with an r-like quality added to the English sounds. (*Shan* is "mountain" in both Old Chinese and modern Mandarin, but its opening sound is, and probably always was, more like the beginning of shred than shed in English.) At the end of a syllable, *h* is a "glottal stop" – the brief catch of breath which in modern Estuary English replaces -t in words like righ', si' (for right, sit).

Ng always represents the single sound of hanger, not the "ngg" sound of anger, even when it occurs at the beginning of a word, as in *ngok*, jade.

There are six simple vowels, written *a*, *e*, *i*, *o*, *ou*, *u*. The first four have their "Continental" values; they are pronounced something like the vowels of pa, pet, pea, pot; and *ou* is used, as in French, for the vowel of pooh. The vowel written *u* was a type of sound that is common in present-day East Asian languages but very rare in European languages (phoneticians call these sounds "back spread vowels"); among the sounds of English, a reasonable substitute for *u* would be the sound which English people write as "er" and Americans as "uh".

The letters -*y* and -*w* after a vowel represent diphthongs beginning with that vowel – *ay* sounds like "eye", *aw* like "ow", *iw* like "ee-oo", *uy* like "er-ee/uh-ee", and so on.

A few words have an *a*- before their first consonant, for instance *atraw* "morning reception" (related to *traw* "morning"). This represents an obscure vowel, as in English attract, but said so briefly that it did not count as a separate syllable.

The acute accent marks a phonetic distinction whose nature is now uncertain. It could have been a contrast of long versus short vowels; alternatively, vowels or diphthongs not marked with an acute may have been said with a slight "y" sound before them. Presence or absence of acute accent does not affect rhyme or metre, so readers who speak the poems aloud can afford to ignore the accents.

Rhyme and rhythm

Poetic structure in these songs depends on regular numbers of syllables, and on rhyme. The rule for rhyming is the same as ours: lines rhyme, if the sounds from the vowel of the last stressed syllable onwards are the same – though a degree of licence was allowed.

Old Chinese is such a "stripped-down" language that there are not many unstressed syllables: most commonly, rhyming syllables are the last syllable of their line. But for instance the grammatical particle *tu* was not stressed. (*Tu* is an all-purpose object pronoun, translatable equally as him, her, it, them; it also forms the possessive, so that *A tu B* corresponds to "A's B" or "the B of A".) Thus in the first song, "The Fish-Hawk's Call", we find *shúh tu* "gather them" rhyming with *wuh tu* "befriend her", and *máwks tu* "reap them" rhyming with *gráwk tu* "delight her" (where the *-s* was evidently not felt to be enough to disallow the rhyme). And, like English folk-songs, Chinese poetry had syllables which were inserted for the sake of rhythm rather than meaning: *i* (pronounced ee), or *uh*. Again, these are irrelevant for rhyme purposes, so for instance in "The Mouse-Ears" we find the last four lines rhyming in *tsa uh* "rocks, oh", *dá uh* "ill, oh", *pha uh* "sick, oh", *wha uh* "sad, oh".

Unstressed syllables are sometimes entirely discounted for the metre. So, in "Please, Second-Son", four-syllable lines in the first two verses are matched in the third verse by the line *ouy nin tu táy ngan*, "I'm afraid of people's gossip" – *nin tu*, "people's", may have been heard as little more than a single syllable. Several common grammar-words consist of a consonant followed by the vowel *u*, which in these cases was probably just a brief obscure vowel: *tu* may have sounded like the second syllable of rota or data (though in English poetry even such brief syllables do count for the metre).

How is Old Chinese reconstructed?

Since Chinese has never been written alphabetically, how do we know how it was pronounced three thousand years ago?

Reconstructing early languages is a science, and, like other scientific enterprises, it assembles diverse lines of evidence and looks for theories consistent with all the data. Many different types of data are relevant for establishing how Chinese was pronounced in the past. This is a highly technical study, and it would not be appropriate to delve into it too deeply here, but the main lines of attack can be indicated.[1]

We can get a fair way back by comparing the modern dialects. Three quarters of the Chinese speak some form of Mandarin, but the remainder, in the south and east, speak five or six non-Mandarin dialects, which are so different from each other that some people prefer to call them separate languages. (In Britain the best-known of these is Cantonese, the domain of which includes Hong Kong.) The period when a unitary Chinese language began to fission into separate dialects

---

[1] I should like to take this opportunity to record my gratitude to the men who trained me in Chinese historical phonology: Edwin Pulleyblank, of Cambridge University and, later, the University of British Columbia, and Hugh Stimson of Yale University.

is commonly thought to be very roughly A.D. 600 (some scholars argue for an earlier date). As it happens, this was about the time when the Chinese compiled "rhyme-books" listing the vocabulary of the language grouped into word-sets with similar pronunciations. The rhyme-books were produced as an aid for poets, and they did not define speech sounds in terms of modern phonetic science (which had not yet been developed either in China or in Europe); but working between the rhyme-book groupings and the various modern dialect pronunciations of words often makes it clear enough what the phonetic realities must have been. The stage of the language reconstructable in this way is called "Middle Chinese".

Because China was so much larger and older a civilization than those of adjacent East Asian peoples, masses of Chinese words were adopted by the languages of the latter. The young civilization of Japan, for instance, borrowed Middle Chinese vocabulary wholesale, and the forms in which these words show up in Japanese give us a cross-check on how they sounded in Chinese at that time.

Something can be learned, too, from loans in the reverse direction. Chinese has not often borrowed words, preferring to coin neologisms from its own stock of roots; but there are exceptions. When Buddhism reached China from India early in our era, various Indian religious terms entered the Chinese language. Many students of Chinese must have shared the surprise I felt when I learned that the Mandarin name for the Buddha is *Fo*. Why *Fo*? The puzzle is solved when one realizes, on the basis of other kinds of evidence already mentioned, that *fo* in modern Mandarin would have been something like *bout* in Middle Chinese. *Bout* may well have been the closest sequence of sounds within Middle Chinese to the Sanskrit *buddha*, and after the name had entered Chinese it would naturally have undergone the same later sound changes as any other Chinese word.

Thus, converging lines of evidence give us rather detailed information on the language as it was roughly a millennium and a half ago. Old Chinese represents another step of comparable length, further into the past.

Here, the most important single category of evidence is the structure of the script. Three thousand years ago, Chinese script was a developing system, and, although not alphabetic, it does contain important clues to pronunciation. The units of the script ("graphs", or "characters") represent words: some words were written as stylized pictures of their meanings, but most words were written by taking a similar-sounding word that already had a graph, and adding an element linked to the meaning of the newly-written word. So the graphs fall into groups sharing a common "phonetic" element: but the words of such a group often sound very different from one another today, and this gives us large hints about sound-changes since the Old Chinese period.

For example, the words for "guest", Mandarin *k'e*, and "road", Mandarin *lu*, are written by adding graphs for "roof" and "foot" respectively to the graph for "each", Mandarin *ke*. *K'e* and *ke* are a reasonable match, but why *lu*? Between Middle Chinese and modern Mandarin these consonants have not changed, so the puzzle is unsolved; but in Old Chinese the words are reconstructed as *kâk* (each), *krhâk* (guest), and *grâks* (road), which do sound rather alike. Regular sound-changes on the way from Old to Middle Chinese, such as apply throughout the history of all languages, happened to turn small phonetic differences into large ones: for instance, the sequence *kr* was simplified to *k* but *gr* was simplified to *r* (which later became *l*).

Another important data source is the *Stu* itself. Later sound-changes have destroyed many rhymes, so the fact that lines were often clearly intended to rhyme guides us towards the pronunciation as it was before the sound-changes applied.

A major source of information about the early history of European languages is comparison of the various branches of the Indo-European language family. Corresponding evidence is less helpful for Chinese: the Sino-Tibetan language family (to which Chinese belongs) is very different from the Indo-European family. Several branches of Indo-European have each led to major world languages documented from early dates; and the branches remained out of contact with one another over long periods, making it easy to tell whether a similarity between words from separate branches genuinely reflects a common origin in the ancestor language (rather than merely representing recent borrowing between languages). On the other hand, apart from Chinese itself the sole Sino-Tibetan languages that are national languages today are Tibetan and Burmese (if Tibet may still be ranked as a nation despite its current subjugation); the earliest records of Tibetan go back only to the sixth century of the Christian era, and of Burmese only to the twelfth century. There are scores, perhaps hundreds, of other Sino-Tibetan languages, but they are spoken by obscure tribal groups and the data on them are inevitably limited. Furthermore, Sino-Tibetan languages tended to remain in mutual contact after they became distinct, muddying the evidence.

Nevertheless, Sino-Tibetan comparisons are relevant. The word for "two", for example, is reconstructed as *nuys* in Old Chinese, which looks fairly different from Middle Chinese *ńźi*, let alone Mandarin *erh*;

but the Old Chinese form looks more plausible alongside *gnyis* in Tibetan, or *nəy* in Bodo (an unwritten Sino-Tibetan language of Assam – the symbol *ə* represents an obscure vowel, not too different from the Old Chinese vowel spelled *u*). And, although the data are scanty, borrowing between languages can be relevant even for the Old Chinese period. Laurent Sagart mentions, for instance, that various non-Chinese languages of the South China area have a word reflecting the Old Chinese word for "lazy": as Chinese colonized the south, this is a word that native work-gangs would have heard often from their Chinese overseers.

Bernhard Karlgren and his successors

The process of marshalling evidence of the kinds discussed in order to reconstruct early stages of Chinese pronunciation was initiated by Chinese scholars during the last, Manchu imperial dynasty (i.e. 1644–1911). Notice, incidentally, that *only* the pronunciation needs to be inferred via scientific hypotheses. The grammar and vocabulary of Old Chinese, too, are very different from those of the modern language, but (unlike in the case of European languages at a comparable date) there is no great mystery about them: we can read Old Chinese.

The Chinese research was brought into relationship with Western phonetic science by the Swede Bernhard Karlgren (1889–1978), who more or less single-handedly established Chinese philology as a discipline in the West. For decades, Karlgren's tabulations of Middle and Old Chinese wordforms were accepted universally as the standard scientific account.

Research continued, though, and in recent years there has been a flowering of studies that take the work of Karlgren and his Chinese predecessors further. A new account of Old Chinese, comparable in scope to Karlgren's, was published by the American William Baxter in 1992. My spellings of Old Chinese words are based on Baxter's system. In some cases I use different letters, in order to avoid special phonetic symbols and make the spellings easier for the general reader; but this is purely a matter of alternative conventions for representing the same sounds – my spellings assume that Baxter's version of Old Chinese pronunciations is correct. (For readers interested in the details, the relationship between Baxter's and my systems is described in the Appendix on pp. 147–50.)

As good luck would have it, Baxter's reconstruction is not only founded on fuller data than were available to Karlgren, but is also aesthetically more pleasing. We cannot expect that distant languages will always sound melodious to Europeans; often they will contain sounds or sound-combinations that strike us as outlandish or downright ugly. Indeed, plenty of English words sound barbaric to French or Italian ears. But Karlgren's version of Old Chinese did seem peculiarly blunt and unpoetic-sounding. One example mentioned by Baxter is a *Stu* line consisting of solemn exclamations, translated as "Oh, alas!" In our version of Old Chinese, the line runs *á-há, úy-tzú!* – which is easy to hear as a lament. If Karlgren's reconstruction were correct, it would instead sound roughly as *o-gho, ur-tzug!* – which is surely less so.

As Baxter rightly says, this is no argument against Karlgren's reconstruction: we cannot be sure what would have sounded solemn to a Chinese of three millennia ago. But we can be grateful that other evidence has led us to move beyond Karlgren's system in some details, because an English-speaking reader would have taken less pleasure in these poems if I had had to use Karlgren's version of Old Chinese. (This is not intended to detract in any way from Karlgren's extraordinary achievements: he was a giant on whose shoulders others are now standing.)

How reliable is the reconstruction?

If an inhabitant of the Chou dynasty could magically return to life, how likely is it that he would recognize this scientific reconstruction as his own language?

Despite my earlier comment about hearing the very sounds used by the *Stu* singers, realistically the most we could hope for is that reconstructed Old Chinese would sound like mangled "foreigner-talk". Someone who tried to speak French from a book, without ever hearing the real thing, could do no better than that. Achieving an authentic accent is far beyond the ambition of an exercise like this one.

Even with respect to the basic consonants and vowels, there must surely be details that are incorrect as they stand. In certain cases we know where the question marks should go. For instance, many words that I spell with an initial *r* are actually reconstructed by Baxter as having an unknown consonant before the *r*. The separate words which I spell alike as *rang* were probably in fact differentiated, as *rang* versus *krang* versus *brang*, say, but since any particular choice of initial consonants would be pure guesswork, it seems better not to choose. Types of evidence that are available for most words will sometimes be lacking for a particular word, making its reconstruction specially doubtful. One example is the word I spell *dzus*, "from". Its meaning ensures that it will never appear in a rhyming position, and the script happens to reveal less about this word than others, so *any* spelling I chose would have involved a large element of guesswork.

In a book intended to further scientific scholarship, guesswork would be inexcusable; the transcriptions would need to contain many ellipsis marks and bracketed letters to show where well-founded hypotheses end and ignorance begins. The results would be unreadable as poetry, so for my intended audience it is necessary to be bolder and less scientific.

Words beginning with *r* are by no means the only words in the poems to have multiple meanings. For instance, *wuh* is listed in the glossary as meaning: right (as opposed to left); to have; a friend; winding. Does this imply that in these other cases, too, the true Old Chinese pronunciations contained additional distinguishing sounds which the reconstruction has missed? No, that does not follow. It is normal for a language to contain "homophones" – in English, "right" means not only right as opposed to left, but also: right as opposed to wrong; an entitlement (I know my rights); immediately (right now); and the same spoken syllable can be write, or rite. The degree of homophony shown in the glossary is not in itself a reason to doubt the Old Chinese reconstruction.

(*After* the Old Chinese period, later Chinese sound-changes produced a massive increase in the number of homophones, which would have made the spoken language unusable if it had not been compensated by large changes in the vocabulary. This is the chief reason why an alphabetic script is unsuitable for modern Chinese. But the number of homophones in Old Chinese as reconstructed looks quite manageable.)

Nevertheless, Baxter's 1992 book is not a final word, any more than Karlgren's system of half a century earlier has proved to be. Baxter and others continue to modify particular features. Laurent Sagart quotes a 1995 Paris lecture by Baxter which argued that certain words must have ended in -*r*; for instance, the word for a spring, which I spell, following the 1992 system, as *sgwan* or *sgwan-ngwan*, would instead have been *sgwar(-ngwar)*.

So, if our version of Old Chinese is just a theoretical structure subject to continuing modification, does that mean that our hypothetically resurrected man of Chou would find our reconstruction of his speech as incomprehensible as he would find English?

I believe not. Scientific progress never reaches a definitive terminus, but future revisions should affect ever-smaller details. My versions of the songs would surely sound somewhat outlandish to our man of Chou, and here and there some particular word would baffle him entirely; but (particularly if he already knew the songs) my guess is that he would recognize the wording. If I did not see that as the balance of probability, I would not have felt this book to be worth compiling. I hope that, for the reader, this is enough.

Editions and interpretations

I have based my translations on a 1971 annotated edition of the *Stu* by Chang Yün-chung. This gives the text of the songs, together with the received interpretations of the various linguistic difficulties they contain.

Inevitably, with such ancient writing that has been studied so intensively, there are many disagreements about the meaning of particular passages; these are conveniently summarized in Bernhard Karlgren's *Glosses on the Book of Odes*, and Karlgren gives his own translations in *The Book of Odes: Chinese Text, Transcription and Translation*. I commonly follow Karlgren's preferred choice among rival interpretations, though here and there I find one of the alternatives better-founded.

Occasionally I impose an interpretation of my own. I give one example, to illustrate the kinds of consideration that arise. The last couplet of "Bamboo Rods" runs: *Kráys ngan thout you / zuh sah ngáyh ou*. The scholarly tradition seems to have taken this without controversy (Karlgren does not gloss the passage) as meaning "Harnessing my carriage I shall go out for an excursion, so as to dissipate my grief".

One objection to this might be that, to a modern mind, it seems bathetic as a response to yearning for a lost love. This is less strong a point than it seems. The Chinese were down-to-earth about love: it mattered to them, as it matters to us, but the idea of love as a grand passion which overwhelms all normal rational considerations was alien. (Arguably, it was unknown to the world at large before it was invented in southern France in the Middle Ages: see for instance my *Brissac and its Mediæval Seigneurs*.) *Stu* poems do sometimes seem to suggest that love troubles are nothing that a brisk country walk cannot cure.

However, there is also a linguistic problem. The word *ngan* is ambiguous between "I, me" and "speech, words"; and the conventional interpretation of *kráys ngan* as "harnessing [my carriage], I ..." reads oddly. Chinese does not require an explicit subject, and if "I" needs to be mentioned here, one wonders why it has been placed so as to split *kráys* from the other two verbs. Logically, under this interpretation, all three of the actions, *kráys* "harness", *thout* "go out", and *you* "wander", should be on a par with one another. To my mind it reads more

21

naturally to take *ngan* as "words", object of *kráys* and subject of the other verbs – and I have translated accordingly, as "I harness words to wander abroad".

But my version could in turn be criticized on the ground that "harnessing words" is too imaginatively metaphorical. In European poetry it would raise no eyebrows, but the *Stu* commonly uses language more literally than that. Questions like this reduce to balances of obscure probabilities, with little chance of definitive resolution.

Emendations to the text

Even the text itself is not beyond question here and there. Some corruptions in the received wording are well recognized. Very occasionally I have allowed myself to make further emendations.

Again "Bamboo Rods" contains an example. The eighth line reads, in Chang Yün-chung's edition, *wants wrhang díh bah múh*, "distancing herself from elder brother(s) and younger brother(s), father and mother". (Old Chinese – and indeed modern Chinese – has no single word for "brother" or for "sister"; different words are used, depending on whether the relative is older or younger.) The Chinese text reprinted in Karlgren's *Book of Odes* had the generations reversed: *wants bah múh wrhang díh*; this destroys the rhyme with *wuh*, "right-hand", in the sixth line, and Karlgren's transliteration into the Roman alphabet exchanges the phrases without comment. But either order gives a five-syllable line in the middle of what are otherwise consistent tetrameters. This is poetically weird – none of the five words are minor grammatical particles which might be discounted for the metre because unstressed. Surely, one of the words (presumably *díh*, "younger brother") must have been inserted by some copyist for whom the usualness of the two-word phrase *wrhang díh* "elder and younger brothers", and the parallel with the phrase *bah múh* "father and mother", weighed heavier than the fact that the resulting line fails to scan. And perhaps, after sound-changes in the language had destroyed the rhymes anyway (the words for "right-hand" and "mother" do not rhyme in Mandarin), another copyist knowingly or unconsciously reversed the phrases to give the senior generation its normal precedence.

The places where I have imposed readings of my own on the text or its interpretation are not many, but where I have done this I do not draw attention to the fact explicitly. Experts on this language and literature will be able to spot my emendations without the help of footnotes, and will judge for themselves whether or not they are justified. Most readers will be more interested in reading poems that work as poems than in these technical philological details.

In the case of song titles, I have felt free to invent my own where convenient. The songs have traditional titles, but these are less a fixed part of the compositions than is usual with European poetry – printed editions of the *Stu* do not always include the titles, and they are very unlikely to have been chosen by the original authors. The traditional titles are commonly formed by mechanically taking the first few content words of the opening line. This can lead to titles that appear quite arbitrary (though distinctive), because the songs often begin with a reference to Nature which serves to set the scene and establish a mood, but has little logical connexion with the main theme. In the first *Stu* song, for instance, the "fish-hawk's call" conjures up the river setting, but plays no part in what follows.

Sometimes it is really impossible to translate the traditional Chinese title for use in English, where titles are assumed to give some clue to the topic. For instance, the song I have entitled "A Jolly Man of the People" has as its Chinese title the single opening word: *mráng*, "population". Accordingly, although my versions use translations of the traditional titles where these "work" in English, where they do not work I have substituted new titles. (The titles in Chinese script, on the other hand, are always the traditional ones.)

The Roman numeral at the foot of each poem identifies it by its place in the fixed traditional sequence of *Stu* poems.

A first step

I should like to end this Introduction with some personal remarks on why this book seemed to me worth producing.

These love songs are one accessible introduction to a civilization which is one of the most complex and most successful that has ever evolved on our planet, and one which, until the last 150 years or less of its three-thousand-year history, was completely untouched by the European-based civilization familiar to most readers.

In the globalized societies of today, it is not easy to learn about sophisticated ways of life that are thoroughly separate from ours. We hear a lot nowadays about multiculturalism and the advantages of diversity. In my experience, those who mouth these slogans loudest tend to be wholly innocent of any real knowledge of cultures other than their own.

This cannot be a healthy state of affairs. I remember that when I graduated in Chinese, forty years ago, I took away from my studies a deep respect and admiration for the civilization of China, and also, through comparison and contrast, a much clearer understanding and valuation than I had before of my own cultural inheritance as an Englishman. As the decades have passed, it has become increasingly clear to me that these lessons – both of them – were the right ones to draw. And they have been joined by consternation at the way that the distinctive approaches to social organization characteristic of my own nation are being eroded or unthinkingly discarded.

Human cultures are not trivial veneers. They are, or can be, deeply different from one another. They are not casually inter-changeable; they vary greatly in the extent to which they satisfy universal human aspirations, and in the purposes which they prioritize at the expense of others. Anyone who has influence over the general nature of his or her society, which under democracy means all of us, needs to understand this. The only way I know to grasp it viscerally as well as just theoretically is to soak oneself in knowledge of a thoroughly separate civilization. Education used to encourage this, via study of the Greeks and Romans. China is arguably a better case, because more separate.

Clearly, reading a collection of ancient love poems could be no more than a tiny first step; but it might be that. Many readers will read these poems for their inherent charm and pass on, and that in itself is good. One or two, though, might perhaps find themselves moved to learn more about traditional China. If so, then they are in for an intellectual feast; and my work in compiling this book will have been richly rewarded.

THE SONGS

Krón, krón, tsa-kou
dzúh gáy tu tou,
íwh-líwh diwk nrah
koun-tzuh hóuh grou.

Shóum-shay gránk shús
tzáyh wuh rou tu,
íwh-líwh diwk nrah
ngás mits grou tu.

Grou tu pu túk
ngás mits sus buk.
Liw tzú, liw tzú!
trent-tront pant juk.

Shóum-shay gránk shús
tzáyh wuh shúh tu,
íwh-líwh diwk nrah
gum sprit wuh tu.

Shóum-shay gránk shús
tzáyh wuh máwks tu,
íwh-líwh diwk nrah
tong káh gráwk tu.

The Fish-Hawk's Call

Krón, krón calls the fish-hawk
on an islet in the river.
A girl who is lovely and good
is the fit match for a princely man.

Unevenly grow the floating-hearts,
to left and right we pick them.
A girl who is lovely and good,
waking and sleeping I search for her.

I search for her but don't find her,
waking and sleeping I brood about her.
Ah, longing! Ah, longing!
Tossing and turning I roll on my side.

Unevenly grow the floating-hearts,
to left and right we gather them.
A girl who is lovely and good,
with lute and harp I'll befriend her.

Unevenly grow the floating-hearts,
to left and right we reap them.
A girl who is lovely and good,
with bells and drums I'll delight her.

I: south of Chou

Floating-hearts, scientifically *Nymphoides*, are river plants like miniature water lilies; their shoots are edible. The "princely man" has for thousands of years been the masculine ideal, a Chinese equivalent to Chaucer's "verray parfit gentil knight". Like our "gentleman", *koun-tzuh* is ambiguous between inherited status and manly behaviour. If the singer is working in a harvesting gang, he can hardly be literally noble; but he can choose to behave as if he were.

Dzenk nrah gu tho,
zhuh ngáyh a deng ngo.
Úts nu pu kéns,
sóu lhouh dre-dro.

Dzenk nrah gu bront,
lu ngáyh lóung kónt.
Lóung kónt wuh wuyh,
lot lak na mruyh.

Dzus muk kwuy lúy,
whín mruyh tsah luks.
Puyh na tu ways mruyh,
mruyh nin tu lu.

The Red Pipe

That demure girl, how sweet she is;
she was going to wait for me by the corner of the town wall.
I love her but I don't see her,
I scratch my head and pace back and forth.

That demure girl, how beautiful she is;
she gave me a red pipe.
Red pipe, you are really bright,
and I delight in your loveliness.

You have come to me like a tendril from the field,
and you are really lovely and unusual;
but it isn't because you are lovely –
it is because a lovely girl gave you to me.

XLII: Púks

The "pipe" may have been a flute; no one knows for sure.

Ké kuts mreng uh,
atraw kuts leng uh.
– Puyh ké tzúk mreng,
sháng-ung tu heng.

Tóng pang mrang uh,
atraw kuts thang uh.
– Puyh tóng pang tzúk mrang,
ngwat thout tu kwáng.

Lroung puy mhúng-mhúng.
– Kám lah tzuh dóng mungs.
– Góps tsah kwuy uh,
mah staks la tzuh tzúng.

Cock-Crow

She: The cock has crowed,
    the court will be filling up!
He: It wasn't the cock crowing,
    it was the buzzing of flies.

She: The East is brightening,
    the court will be swept and garnished!
He: It isn't the East brightening,
    it is the light of the Moon rising.

She: Crowds of insects are on the wing!
He: It is sweet dreaming alongside you.
She: The assembly will reconvene soon;
    we don't want them being malicious about the two of us.

XCVI: Atsúy

31

Púk poum gu grang,
wah sot gu pháng.
Wéts nu hóus ngáyh,
wé nhouh dóng gráng.
Gu kha, gu za,
kuts kuk teh tza.

Púk poum gu krúy,
wah sot gu phuy.
Wéts nu hóus ngáyh,
wé nhouh dóng kwuy.
Gu kha, gu za,
kuts kuk teh tza.

Mák khak puyh gwá,
mák mhúk puyh á.
Wéts nu hóus ngáyh,
wé nhouh dóng ka.
Gu kha, gu za,
kuts kuk teh tza.

The North Wind

The north wind is so chill,
the sleet is so thick.
If you are sweet and love me,
I'll hold your hand and go with you.
– He is so shy, he is so slow,
but it is urgent now!

The north wind is so cold,
the sleet is so heavy.
If you are sweet and love me,
I'll hold your hand and you can take me home.
– He is so shy, he is so slow,
but it is urgent now!

The only red to see is foxes,
the only black to see is crows.
If you are sweet and love me,
I'll hold your hand and get in your carriage.
– He is so shy, he is so slow,
but it is urgent now!

XLI: Púks

Láts ka gámp-gámp
tswats uy na lhámp.
Khúyh pu nayh sus,
ouy tzuh pu kámp.

Láts ka thóun-thóun
tswats uy na móun.
Khúyh pu nayh sus,
ouy tzuh pu póun.

Kók tzúk luks stit,
sih tzúk dóng wít.
Wuts tzuh pu snins,
wuh na kéw nit!

The Big Carriage

My big carriage rumbles,
my patterned robe is like young silvergrass.
How can I not long for you,
but I'm afraid you won't dare.

My big carriage roars,
my patterned robe is like red millet.
How can I not long for you,
but I'm afraid you won't run away with me.

While we live you shall have your own room,
when we die we shall share one grave.
If you say I am not to be trusted:
by the bright sun, I am!

LXXIII: Royal Domain

Lhámp is said to refer to Chinese silvergrass (*Miscanthus*) in its young, unwithered state. This is a plant often grown ornamentally – its leaves catch the light to create an impression of cool green shot through with silver. Red millet, likewise, is a showy variety. The roaring and rumbling was road noise rather than a motor, but the idea of big cars and smart clothes as routes to a girl's heart is a familiar one.

Finding English words for the men's clothes mentioned in these poems is rather difficult, because traditional Chinese dress was different from ours. The main elements, for either sex, were the *dang*, which wrapped round the body and in particular covered the legs in the manner of a skirt, and the *uy*, which covered the upper body in the manner of a jacket. Both sexes held their clothes together with a sash or belt (*gums*, or *táts*). I do not know whether trousers existed at all at this early period, but more recently trousers were associated specifically with manual workers (men or women). If we wished to use consistent translations for Chinese *uy* and *dang*, the obvious words would be jacket and skirt, but it gives a strange impression in English if, for instance, a woman comments admiringly on her male lover's skirt. To avoid these difficulties, I have tended to use vague words such as "robe".

Shúh shúh kront-nuh
pu leng kwheng-kwhang.
Tzay ngáyh gróuy nin,
tris payh Tiw gráng.

Tuk payh sdóuy-ngóuy
ngáyh mráh hóuy-lóuy.
Ngáyh ká tawk payh krum róuy,
wi zuh pu wrank gróuy.

Tuk payh káw káng
ngáyh mráh gwín-akwáng.
Ngáyh ká tawk payh zih kwráng,
wi zuh pu wrank lhang.

Tuk payh tsa uh,
ngáyh mráh dá uh,
ngáyh bók pha uh,
wun gáy wha uh!

The Mouse-Ears

Reaping the mouse-ears,
I am not filling my slanted-basket.
Alas, my beloved,
they have sent him on the Chou road.

I'd go up that crag,
but my horse is worn out.
I'll just pour wine into this golden jar,
to stop my endless yearning.

I'd go up that high ridge,
but my horse has the black-and-yellow sickness.
I'll just pour wine into this rhinoceros horn,
to stop my endless grieving.

I'd go up those rocks, oh,
but my horse is ill, oh,
my driver is sick, oh,
how sad I am, oh!

III: south of Chou

Kront-nuh, literally "rolled ears", is the Chinese name for the edible plant mouse-ear chickweed (*Cerastium vulgatum*). A *kwheng-kwhang*, literally "slanted-basket", was used in harvesting.

The Chou road was the road to the dynastic capital, so a young man sent that way had been taken to serve, probably as a soldier. The singer hopes that if she can get to the top of the hill she might see him returning.

Mráng tu thu-thu,
bóuh pás mrós su;
puyh rú mrós su,
rú tzik ngáyh mu.
Sóngs tzuh dap Gu,
tits wa Tóuns kwhu.
Puyh ngáyh krhan gru,
tzuh mah rang mú.
Tsang tzuh mah nah,
tsiw zuh way gru.

Lung pay kwayh wan
zuh mangs bouk krón.
Pu kéns bouk krón,
krhup thíh ran-ran;
kuts kéns bouk krón,
tzúks saws tzúks ngan.
Nayh pók nayh gets,
rhíh mah gouh ngan;
zuh nayh ka rú,
zuh ngáyh hóuy tsan.

Sáng tu mouts grák,
gu lap áwk nak.
Wha tzay, kou i,
mah luk sáng sgoump!
Wha tzay, nrah i,
mah lah ashuh tóum!
Ashuh tu tóum i,
you kháyh lhot lay;
nrah tu tóum i,
pu kháyh lhot lay.

Sáng tu grák i,
gu akwáng nu wrun.
Dzus ngáyh dzá nayh,
sóum swat luk brun.
Gu lhouyh lhang-lhang,

38

A Jolly Man of the People

You were a jolly man of the people,
bringing funds to buy silk;
but you had not come to buy silk:
once you arrived it was me you were after.
We went paddling in the Gu river together,
we went all the way to Tóuns hill.
It was not I who delayed things;
you had no satisfactory go-between.
I begged you not to be angry,
and we fixed the date for autumn.

I would climb that ruined wall,
to watch for you returning to the town gate.
If I did not see you coming to the gate,
my tears fell, drop after drop;
once I had seen you come to the gate,
then I was laughing, then I was talking.
I cast your omens by turtle-shell and by milfoil-stalk,
and they contained nothing worrying.
You arrived with your carriage;
I moved house with my valuables.

While the mulberries remain unwithered,
the leaves are so glossy.
Ah, pigeons!
Don't eat the mulberry fruit.
Ah, women!
Don't take your pleasure with men.
If a man takes his pleasure,
that can always be excused.
If a woman takes her pleasure,
that is inexcusable.

When the mulberry leaves wither,
they go yellow and fall.
From the time I came to you,
for three years I have tasted poverty.
The Gu river is in spate,

39

tzam ka wi dang.
Nrah lay pu shank:
ashuh nuys gu gang.
Ashuh lay mank guk,
nuys sóum gu túk.

Sóum swat way buh,
mayh stit ráw uh;
souk hung yaks mits,
mayh wuh atraw uh.
Ngan kuts zouts uh,
tits a báwks uh;
wrhang díh pu tre,
dít gu saws uh.
Dzenk ngan sus tu,
kroung dzus dáwks uh.

Gup nayh krí róuh,
róuh shuh ngáyh ons.
Gu tzúk wuh ngans,
zup tzúk wuh pháns.
Tzóng krók tu króns,
ngan saws ráns-ráns,
snins dats táns-táns;
pu su gu pant:
pant deh pu su.
Ak luh an tzú.

The language here is fairly straightforward, but some cultural references need explanation. *Pás*, in the second line, is literally "cloth", but at this period cloth was used as a currency – metal coins had not yet been introduced. The delicate matter of arranging a marriage depended crucially, then and much more recently in Chinese history, on the services of a go-between neutral between the two families.

The river Gu is mentioned in several of these poems: there is a problem about identifying it. The river which bears the name today is a minor tributary of another river named after the large Chou-dynasty State through whose former territory it runs (and where this poem was collected), namely Wrats. (On Western maps the names Gu and Wrats are of course written in their modern Mandarin forms, which are Ch'i and Wei respectively.) The Gu which these singers knew seems to have been a more important river. My assumption (I can find no discussion of the point in any reference book) is that, 2,700 years

it soaks the bottom of my carriage curtains.
Myself, I was not disloyal,
but your behaviour was two-faced.
You: you were utterly deceitful,
your character quite unreliable.

For three years I was your wife,
I didn't treat the housework as a burden.
I got up early and went to bed in the dark,
with no mornings relaxing with friends.
I kept my promises,
but you came to violence.
My brothers do not understand,
their laughter is scornful;
Though I talk demurely, I brood over it,
feeling sorry for myself.

The two of us were to grow old together,
but age led you to resent me.
Even the Gu river has a further bank,
even a swamp has a far side!
While my hair was bound up in girl's tufts
I talked and laughed happily,
I swore earnest oaths of sincerity.
I had no thought that things could go wrong.
Going wrong, this I had no thought of.
But ah, all that is over now.

LVIII: Wrats

ago, the name Gu must have been used for the whole river of which the
present-day Gu is a tributary – or, more precisely (since movements of the
Yellow River have led to large changes in other rivers of North China), that the
Chou-dynasty Gu was a river whose nearest present-day equivalent is the
Wrats.

The word *zup* in the last verse occurs in many of these poems; it is hard to
translate, because Chinese rivers were often different from the managed
watercourses we know in the 21st century, with clear streams flowing swiftly
between neatly-defined banks. A river in Chou China would often be a broad
expanse within which the moving stream itself might be lost among a congeries
of boggy ground, standing pools, backwaters, and islets of different degrees of
firmness. All this low, wet ground was *zup*, in contrast to the slopes or hills – I
translate it here as "swamp", but in other contexts "wet ground" or "river-
bank" might be better choices. *Continued overleaf...*

41

Koun-tzuh wa wek:
pu tre gu gru;
akát tits tzú?
Ké súy wa du;
nit tu zak uh,
ngwu yang gráh rú.
Koun-tzuh wa wek,
na tu gáy mout su?

Koun-tzuh wa wek:
pu nit, pu ngwat;
akát gu wuh gwát?
Ké súy wa grat;
nit tu zak uh,
ngwu yang gráh kwát.
Koun-tzuh wa wek,
króh mah kruy khát!

Continued from previous page:

Turtle shells and milfoil stalks were standard tools for foretelling the future in early China. With shells (ox shoulderblades were also used), a heated metal point was used to crack the surface, and the pattern of cracks gave the answer to the question. Lengths of milfoil stalk which were either jointed or smooth represented the Yin and Yang principles; a set of such lengths was shuffled in a ritual fashion to yield one of the 64 hexagrams whose occult interpretations are listed in the Chinese *Book of Changes* (in Mandarin, *I Ching*). The eight trigrams which paired off to give 64 hexagrams can be seen today surrounding the Yin–Yang symbol on the flag of South Korea.

From our point of view, these techniques are superstitious – meaning that we know, now, that they do not work. In the Chou dynasty, they were reasonable attempts to make sense of a mysterious and difficult world. We should not feel too scornful about shell-and-bone divination, in particular, because our knowledge of the beginning of written Chinese is entirely dependent on it. When a question was put to the oracle, it was written on the shell or bone, and the response as interpreted from the cracks was written alongside it. The earliest surviving examples of Chinese writing, dating from about 1200 B.C. onwards, are all instances of this divination technique.

A Chinese child's hair is standardly bound up into two tufts, called in Old Chinese *króns*.

My man has been called up

My man has been called up:
I don't know when his release will be
– oh, when will it come?
The fowls go to roost in their nest-holes;
it is the evening of the day,
and the sheep and cattle come down from the pasture.
But my man has been called up
– how can I fail to think about him?

My man has been called up:
not just for days, not just for months
– when will he rejoin me?
The fowls go to roost on their perches;
it is the evening of the day,
and the sheep and cattle gather from the hillside.
But my man has been called up
– oh, don't let him be hungry or thirsty!

LXVI: Royal Domain

Here, a wife uses *koun-tzuh*, "princely man", to refer to her husband who has been taken for military service. From an English-speaking wife, "my prince" might sound sarcastic, while "my master" has a servile connotation that would seem out of place to us (though not to a Chou-dynasty Chinese). So I have translated the phrase neutrally as "my man".

A farmstead was surrounded by simple earthen walls in which it was easy to scoop out holes for hens to roost in. These holes were called *du*.

Wan shúh gláng uh,
Múts tu hangs uh,
wun douy tu su?
Mruyh mrángs Kang uh!
Gru ngáyh á sáng kloung,
ew ngáyh á dangs koung,
sóngs ngáyh á Gu tu dangs uh.

Wan shúh mrúk uh,
Múts tu púk uh,
wun douy tu su?
Mruyh mrángs Luk uh!
Gru ngáyh á sáng kloung,
ew ngáyh á dangs koung,
sóngs ngáyh á Gu tu dangs uh.

Wan shúh phong uh,
Múts tu tóng uh,
wun douy tu su?
Mruyh mrángs Long uh!
Gru ngáyh á sáng kloung,
ew ngáyh á dangs koung,
sóngs ngáyh á Gu tu dangs uh.

Among the Mulberry Trees

Pulling up dodder
to the south of Múts,
pray who am I thinking about?
It's the lovely eldest daughter of the Kang family!
She made a date with me among the mulberry trees,
she met me at the upper temple,
she walked out with me along the river Gu.

Harvesting wheat
to the north of Múts,
pray who am I thinking about?
It's the lovely eldest daughter of the Luk family!
She made a date with me among the mulberry trees,
she met me at the upper temple,
she walked out with me along the river Gu.

Pulling up turnips
to the east of Múts,
pray who am I thinking about?
It's the lovely eldest daughter of the Long family!
She made a date with me among the mulberry trees,
she met me at the upper temple,
she walked out with me along the river Gu.

XLVIII: Long

Dodder is a parasitic weed that has to be removed from crops early in the growing season, before it can destroy their food value. Wheat is harvested in summer. Root vegetables like turnips are lifted when the cold weather has arrived.

Tóng mún tu lang,
gu lap tzáng-tzáng.
Mrun zuh way gru,
Mrang Séng wáng-wáng.

Tóng mún tu lang,
gu lap phóts-phóts.
Mrun zuh way gru,
Mrang Séng tats-tats.

The Poplar by the East Gate

The poplar by the East Gate,
its leaves are thick.
Sundown was the time we agreed;
now the Evening Star is gleaming.

The poplar by the East Gate,
its leaves are dense.
Sundown was the time we agreed;
now the Evening Star is brilliant.

CXL: Drin

The lady has not shown up.

Zhuh ngáyh a dra, á-nu;
thong nuh zuh sáks, á-nu;
dangs tu zuh gweng wrhá, á-nu.

Zhuh ngáyh a léng, á-nu;
thong nuh zuh shéng, á-nu;
dangs tu zuh gweng wréng, á-nu.

Zhuh ngáyh a dáng, á-nu;
thong nuh zuh akwáng, á-nu;
dangs tu zuh gweng rang, á-nu.

Within the Gate-Screen

He waited for me within the gate-screen, so he did;
His ear-stoppers were white, so they were;
On them he wore flower-shaped jewels, so he did.

He waited for me in the courtyard, so he did;
His ear-stoppers were green, so they were;
On them he wore *wréng* gems, so he did.

He waited for me in the hall, so he did;
His ear-stoppers were yellow, so they were;
On them he wore blossom-shaped jewels, so he did.

XCVIII: Atsúy

The gateway between a private compound and the outside world would have a small screening wall built directly inside it, not necessarily to guard against violent attack but for privacy and to avoid giving evil spirits easy access. The *dra* was the area between the gate and the screening wall.

The Introduction mentioned that this volume includes most but not all of the *Stu* songs with a love theme. This song certainly describes a lady receiving her lover or fiancé, who meets her closer to her own chamber in successive verses; I offer it here as a representative example of the group of songs I was minded to omit.

One problem for the modern reader is that we do not know much about the "ear-stoppers" (if indeed that is a suitable translation). We know from many sources that ornamental earplugs of some kind were an important part of dress in the Chou dynasty, but exactly what they looked like and what function they served is mysterious – was it indecent to display naked earholes? Already by the time of the Han Dynasty (about the time of Christ) the Chinese commentators were discussing this topic in a bewildered fashion. (We also do not know precisely how the jewels mentioned should be translated.)

Even without these puzzles, though, there might be a certain flatness about this poem. It must be for the reader to judge whether this would have been a better book, if the poems it does contain were interspersed with two or three dozen comparable to this one.

Tsang Gloungs-tzuh i,
mah lo ngáyh ruh,
mah tat ngáyh dos khuh!
Khúyh kámp úts tu,
ouy ngáyh bah múh.
Gloungs kháyh gróuy lay;
bah múh tu ngan,
ak kháyh ouy lay.

Tsang Gloungs-tzuh i,
mah lo ngáyh dzang,
mah tat ngáyh dos sáng!
Khúyh kámp úts tu,
ouy ngáyh ta wrhang.
Gloungs kháyh gróuy lay;
ta wrhang tu ngan,
ak kháyh ouy lay.

Tsang Gloungs-tzuh i,
mah lo ngáyh wan,
mah tat ngáyh dos dán!
Khúyh kámp úts tu,
ouy nin tu táy ngan.
Gloungs kháyh gróuy lay;
nin tu táy ngan,
ak kháyh ouy lay.

Please, Second-Son

Please, Second-Son,
don't trespass into our compound,
don't break the matrimony-vines we planted.
Of course I don't care about them,
but I'm afraid of my parents.
Second-Son is lovable,
but the words of my parents:
they are something to fear.

Please, Second-Son,
don't trespass through our wall,
don't break the mulberries we planted.
Of course I don't care about them,
but I'm afraid of my brothers.
Second-Son is lovable,
but the words of my brothers:
they are something to fear.

Please, Second-Son,
don't trespass into our garden,
don't break the sandalwood-trees we planted.
Of course I don't care about them,
but I'm afraid of people's gossip.
Second-Son is lovable,
but people's gossip:
that is something to fear.

LXXVI: Dengs

The matrimony-vine or boxthorn (*Lycium chinense*) is a shrub which can be grown as a hedge, and has many medicinal and other uses.

Koun-tzuh krí róuh,
phuks kí rouk kráy;
oy-oy-láy-láy,
na shan na gáy,
zank buk deh ngay.
Tzuh tu pu diwk,
wun na tu gáy?

Tseyh i, tseyh i
gu tu léwk lay.
Tint pot na wun,
pu sít léks lay.
Ngok tu thín lay!
Zank tu théks lay!
Lang tza tu sék lay!
Gá-nan nu lhín lay,
gá-nan nu téks lay?

Tsáyh i, tsáyh i
gu tu trants lay,
móng pay jos thi,
deh lat ban lay.
Tzuh tu tseng lang!
Lang tza tu ngrán lay!
Trent na tu nin i
próng tu wrans lay.

According to some of the commentators, this song is satirical: it mocks a specific historical figure, the lady Swan Kang, who was beautiful but was indeed not good. Swan Kang was a noblewoman of Atsúy who was betrothed to Kup-tzuh, son and heir to the ruler of Wrats; but after coming to Wrats to be married, she instead married the ruler himself, and drove his first wife to suicide. Then later, when Swan Kang had sons of her own, she conspired with one of them to have Kup-tzuh killed, enabling her son to succeed to the throne.

Utterly Submissive

The prince's consort:
the hairpin in her headdress bears six gems;
she is utterly submissive;
she is majestic as the hills and the river;
the figured dress is right for her.
For her not to be good,
pray, how could that be?

Bright, shining bright
is her pheasant feather.
Her black hair is like the clouds,
she scorns false hair.
Her earstoppers of jade!
Her hairpin of ivory!
The whiteness of her forehead!
How can she be so celestial?
How can she be such a goddess?

White, gleaming white
is her ritual robe,
it covers the crushed linen,
that is her plain undergarment.
Her clear forehead!
The colour of her forehead!
Truly, a woman like this
is the belle of the nation.

XLVII: Long

In "A Jolly Man of the People" we saw that *krí róuh*, literally "grow old together", was a conventional way of referring to marriage. In the first line here, the phrase is used as a noun – the one with whom one grows old together, i.e. one's life-partner. The phrase *koun-tzuh* may refer to Kup-tzuh, literally the ruler's son, alongside whom Swan Kang was intended to grow old. Across the border in the State of Long, it was perhaps safe to comment satirically on events in neighbouring Wrats.

Kloung kók wuh thóuy,
hánt gu kán uh.
Wuh nrah phih ray,
khúts gu nhán uh.
Khúts gu nhán uh,
ngos nin tu krún náns uh.

Kloung kók wuh thóuy,
hánt gu sliw uh.
Wuh nrah phih ray,
líw gu síws uh.
Líw gu síws uh,
ngos nin tu pu diwk uh.

Kloung kók wuh thóuy,
hánt gu khup uh.
Wuh nrah phih ray,
trot gu krhup uh.
Trot gu krhup uh,
gáy tzay gup uh?

Parched Motherwort

In the middle of the valley there is motherwort;
its dry stems are scorched.
There is a girl who has been sent away;
her sighs are sad.
Her sighs are sad,
encountering human misery.

In the middle of the valley there is motherwort;
its withered stems are scorched.
There is a girl who has been sent away;
her wailing is long-drawn-out.
Her wailing is long-drawn-out,
encountering human wickedness.

In the middle of the valley there is motherwort;
its parched stems are scorched.
There is a girl who has been sent away;
her sobs are convulsive.
Her sobs are convulsive,
but where will "alas" get her?

LXIX: Royal Domain

Motherwort, *Leonurus cardiaca*, is a weed of the mint family which grows a few feet tall. If it is parched even in the middle of the valley, where water should normally flow, this must be a bad season with a poor harvest expected. This has led some commentators to suggest that the girl is a servant who has been turned out because her master cannot keep her on. But that implies an abnormally close link between the opening lines and the main theme. *Stu* poems very often begin with an image drawn from Nature, but commonly these images function just to establish a mood. (We shall see cases where it is hard to grasp how they do even that.) There is no assumption that the opening "scene-setting" reference is an integral part of the story. Surely, here, the girl has been rejected by a husband or lover, not by an employer.

It might seem excessive to translate *pu diwk*, literally "not good", as "wicked". But in fact even in modern Chinese the concept "bad" is standardly expressed in this roundabout way. Stalin or Hitler in Mandarin would be *hen pu hao jen*, "very not good men".

Bou-you tu wrah,
uy-dang chah-chah.
Sum tu ou uh,
a ngáyh kwuy khah.

Bou-you tu luk,
shúh-shúh uy-buk.
Sum tu ou uh,
a ngáyh kwuy suk.

Bou-you got lot,
mráy uy na sot.
Sum tu ou uh,
a ngáyh kwuy lhots.

The Mayfly

Like the mayfly's wings,
your dress is splendid.
My heart is so sad,
come home with me.

Like the wings of the mayfly,
your clothes are brightly coloured.
My heart is so sad,
come and sleep with me.

Like the mayfly bursting forth from its hole,
your hempen robe is as the snow.
My heart is so sad,
come and spend the night with me.

CL: Dzóu

After it emerges in its adult form, the mayfly mates and dies within a single day. This young man seems to be hoping for a similarly short-term relationship.

Wuh ka rin-rin,
wuh mráh brák tín.
Mouts kéns koun-tzuh,
sdus-nin tu lin.

Pant wuh tsit,
zup wuh rit.
Kuts kéns koun-tzuh,
benk dzóyh káh sprit.
Kum tah póut gráwk,
dats tah gu dít.

Pant wuh sáng,
zup wuh lang.
Kuts kéns koun-tzuh,
benk dzóyh káh gwáng.
Kum tah póut gráwk,
dats tah gu mang.

Rumbling Carriages

Carriages are rumbling,
there are horses with silver blazes.
I have not seen my lord yet;
I give orders to the servant.

On the slopes there are lacquer-trees,
on the river-bank there are chestnuts.
When I have seen my lord,
we shall sit together playing the harp.
If we do not enjoy ourselves today,
in the future old age awaits.

On the slopes there are mulberries,
on the river-bank there are poplars.
When I have seen my lord,
we shall sit together playing the flute.
If we do not enjoy ourselves today,
in the future we shall be gone.

CXXVI: Dzin

On one interpretation, the singer is trying to convince herself that the great
man is as interested in seeing her again as she is in seeing him.

Zup wuh drang-chah,
ayh-nayh gu ke,
aw tu áwk-áwk.
Gráwk tzuh tu mah tre.

Zup wuh drang-chah,
ayh-nayh gu wrhá,
aw tu áwk-áwk.
Gráwk tzuh tu mah krá.

Zup wuh drang-chah,
ayh-nayh gu lit,
aw tu áwk-áwk.
Gráwk tzuh tu mah stit.

Starfruit Trees on the River Bank

There are starfruit trees on the river bank,
luxuriant are their branches,
glossy with youth.
I am delighted that you have no boyfriend.

There are starfruit trees on the river bank,
luxuriant are their blossoms,
glossy with youth.
I am delighted that you are not the lady of a house.

There are starfruit trees on the river bank,
luxuriant are their fruit,
glossy with youth.
I am delighted that you have no married-woman's chamber.

CXLVIII: Kwóts

The singer hopes to supply the deficiencies himself.
Starfruit tree (carambola) is one theory about the identity of the trees described.

Bewh wuh mú,
gu lit tsit i.
Grou ngáyh staks ashuh,
lúh gu kit i.

Bewh wuh mú,
gu lit sóum i.
Grou ngáyh staks ashuh,
lúh gu kum i.

Bewh wuh mú,
kwheng-kwhang huts tu.
Grou ngáyh staks ashuh,
lúh gu wuts tu.

The Plum Tree is Shedding

The plum-tree is shedding,
its fruit are seven.
Various gentlemen are courting me,
may good fortune arrive.

The plum-tree is shedding,
its fruit are three.
Various gentlemen are courting me,
may the time arrive.

The plum-tree is shedding,
I gather the plums in my slanted basket.
Various gentlemen are courting me,
may a proposal arrive.

XX: south of Daws

Bróu wuh kháh lap,
tzúys wuh lhum dap.
Lhum tzúk rats,
tsant tzúk krhats.

Wuh meyh tzúys leng,
wuh louyh lih mreng.
Tzúys leng pu no kwrouh,
lih mreng grou gu mouh.

Ong, ong, mreng ngráns,
hos nit lhuh táns;
ashuh na kwuy tsúy,
lúh prung muts pháns.

Taw-taw tou-tzuh,
nin dap, ngáng puh.
Nin dap, ngáng puh,
ngáng so ngáyh wuh.

The Gourd Has its Bitter Leaves

The gourd has its bitter leaves,
the ford has deep wading.
Where it is deep it is wetting people's clothes,
where it is shallow they are lifting up their skirts.

Abundant flows are filling up the ford,
the hen-pheasant is calling, cry upon cry.
The depth in the ford is not yet up to the carriage-axles;
the hen-pheasant is calling for her mate.

Ong, ong calls the wild goose,
the warm sun is just rising.
If the man is to come back to his wife,
it should be when the ice has not yet melted.

The boatman is beckoning,
people are crossing, but not me.
People are crossing, but not me:
I wait for my beloved.

XXXIV: Púks

The gourd being in leaf, the ice melted, and the pheasant calling all show that the season is advanced past the point when her man should have come for her; but the water is not too deep yet, it is still possible.

    The wild goose to the Chinese symbolizes solitude.

Zoup zoup kók poum,
zuh oum zuh wah;
mrunt-mrant dóng sum,
pu ngay wuh nah.
Shúh phong shúh phuyh,
mah zuh gráh rhíh;
túk um mák wuy,
gup nayh dóng sih.

Gráng lóuh druy-druy,
kloung sum wuh wuy;
pu want ruy nuyh,
ba sóngs ngáyh guy.
Douy wuts lá kháh?
Gu kám na dzúyh.
Ráns nayh sin mrun,
na wrhang na dúyh.

Kéng zuh Wuts drók,
sduk-sduk gu tuh;
ráns nayh sin mrun,
pu ngáyh sít zuh.
Ma dats ngáyh rang,
ma pát ngáyh kóh!
Ngáyh kroung pu lot,
wáng swit ngáyh wóh.

Dzous gu lhum uh,
pang tu, tou tu;
dzous gu tsant uh,
wrangs tu, you tu.
Gáy wuh, gáy mang?
Mrunt-mrant grou tu.
Bom min wuh smáng,
ba-buk kous tu.

The East Wind

Zoup, zoup gusts the East wind
with clouds and with rain;
I strive to make my heart agreeable,
it is not right to harbour anger.
Harvesting turnips or radishes
one cannot check what their body will be like.
My reputation is unsullied;
I am with you until death.

But I go my road haltingly
and in my heart there is rebellion.
Not far, just a little way,
you trailed to the door with me.
Who says the dandelion is bitter?
It is sweet as shepherd's-purse.
You are feasting your new bride,
you and your brothers.

The Wuts river is turbulent when the Kéng river joins it,
but then it slows down and becomes clear.
You are feasting your new bride,
and you don't think I am wholesome.
Don't you touch me down there, then!
Don't you grope my quim!
If my body is unpleasing
I'll devote my time to our children.

When we reached deep water
we got through on a raft or a boat;
when we came to where it was shallow
we waded, or we swam.
What did we have, what did we lack?
I strove to supply our needs.
If any of our people had a bereavement
I crawled on my knees to help them.

Pu ngáyh nú houk,
pant zuh ngáyh way gou;
kuts jah ngáyh túk,
káh longs pu dous.
Sak louk khonk kouk,
gup nayh tín phouk;
kuts sheng kuts louk,
bih la wa dóuk.

Ngáyh wuh kih hrouk,
ak zuh ngrás tóung;
ráns nayh sin mrun,
zuh ngayh ngrás goung.
Wuh kwáng wuh góuts,
kuts lu ngáyh lups;
pu níms sak tah,
ruy la rú huts.

Marriage is for life, and one cannot know how a spouse will turn out any more than one knows what the body of a root vegetable will be like before one pulls it out of the ground. But a Chinese man who could afford it was free to take additional, younger wives.

Although the overall tenor of this poem is clear, some individual passages are generally recognized to be obscure. The lines I translate "Not far, just a little way ..." seem to refer to the polite Chinese custom of going part of the way on the road with someone who departs: this husband accompanied the singer for the bare minimum distance. But it seems unlikely that the wife of long standing has literally been turned out of her home to wander the roads. Perhaps she was demoted to less desirable quarters within the family compound, and the husband was dismissive about the new arrangements; or possibly the "door" is purely metaphorical.

Dandelion and shepherd's-purse look rather similar (before they flower, at least – shepherd's-purse has tiny white flowers). Shepherd's-purse is thoroughly edible, and rather pretty with its heart-shaped seed cases; in East Asia it is cultivated for food even today. Dandelion leaves certainly can be eaten, in salads for instance, but it is less sought-after as a food plant. The comparison with new and old wives is clear.

The Old Chinese *lá* stood for dandelions (together with plants such as sowthistle, which to a non-botanist look much the same). But when the tea plant was introduced to China from South-East Asia, a thousand years after the time of our poems, the word changed its reference to mean "tea". Indeed, the

You did not look after me or cherish me –
on the contrary, you treated me as an enemy;
now that you have cast aspersions on my virtue
a merchant could not even sell me as a concubine.
In the old days, growing up, I was scared and impoverished,
I joined you and we were destitute;
now I have lived and grown up,
and you compare me to poison.

I keep a fine larder
to get us through the winter;
but you are feasting your new bride,
and I am just your guarantee against hunger.
You are fierce and violent,
and your only gift to me has been toil.
You don't remember the old days,
when it was me you came to for rest.

XXXV: Púks

English word tea, and the colloquial "char", both ultimately derive, via some large sound-changes, from this same Old Chinese word *lá*. Probably, the Chinese had been drinking infusions of dandelion or sowthistle leaves, before they discovered a better alternative.

The lines about rivers flowing together plainly mean that the man is in a frenzy of sexual excitement which will not last. (It is interesting to find a song gathered in the State of Púks referring to rivers far away in the original Chou heartland.) The passage about rafts, wading, and so on is more obscure. The singer is perhaps reminding the husband how, when he was young and poor, the two of them managed as a team to deal with whatever life threw at them.

Krat-krat kán máw
dzúh Souns tu kráw.
Sáks su bis tu,
rang mráh sits tu.
Payh tho tah tzuh,
gáy zuh pits tu?

Krat-krat kán la
dzúh Souns tu tá.
Sáks su tzáh tu,
rang mráh ngáh tu.
Payh tho tah tzuh,
gáy zuh lah tu?

Krat-krat kán tzeng
dzúh Souns tu deng.
Sáks su touk tu,
rang mráh rouk tu.
Payh tho tah tzuh,
gáy zuh kóuks tu?

The Ox-Tail Pennon

Aloft on its pole is the ox-tail pennon
in the outskirts of Souns.
It is braided with white silk;
fine horses there are four.
This open-hearted gentleman,
what can I give him?

Aloft on its pole is the falcon flag
within the outer wall of Souns.
It is corded with white silk;
fine horses there are five.
This open-hearted gentleman,
what can I present to him?

Aloft on its pole is the feather-pennon
within the inner wall of Souns.
It is bound with white silk;
fine horses there are six.
This open-hearted gentleman,
what can I say to him?

LIII: Long

Instead of oblong flags bearing the abstract designs of European heraldry, the
arrival of a great man in China was advertised by displays of animal trophies.
According to James Legge, the first translator of the *Stu* into English, a *máw*
was a pole "adorned with feathers. It was carved with the figure of some
animal, or had such a figure set upon it; and the pennon hung down, consisting
of ox-tails, dressed and strung together". A *tzeng* was similar "but instead of the
ox-tails, the pennon was composed of feathers of different colours, skilfully
disposed in spreading plumes". Legge explains the growing number of horses by
suggesting that they are those of dignitaries of Souns gathering to welcome the
visitor.

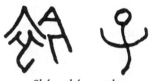

Shéng-shéng tzuh gums,
liw-liw ngáyh sum.
Tsongs ngáyh pu wank,
tzuh néng pu zus um?

Shéng-shéng tzuh bús,
liw-liw ngáyh su.
Tsongs ngáyh pu wank,
tzuh néng pu rú?

Klháw i, lhát i,
dzúh deng kwhat i.
It nit pu kéns
na sóum ngwat i.

The Green Sash

Green, green is your sash,
longing, longing is my heart.
True, I am making no move towards you,
but why do you send no more messages to me?

Green, green are your netsuke,
longing, longing are my thoughts.
True, I am making no move towards you,
but why do you not come to me?

Pacing back and forth, oh,
on the town lookout tower, oh,
one day not seeing you
is like three months, oh.

XCI: Dengs

Chinese robes had no pockets; a man hung his kit on short cords from his sash
or belt, using toggles to stop the cords slipping through. The toggles were
traditionally carved from jade and might be little works of art in their own
right; Western collectors refer to them by their Japanese name, *netsuke*.

Lhéwk-lhéwk trouk kán
zuh téws wa Gu.
Khúyh pu nayh su?
Want mák trits tu.

Sgwan-ngwan dzúh tzáyh,
Gu lhouyh dzúh wuh.
Nrah-tzuh wuh gráng,
wants wrhang bah múh.

Gu lhouyh dzúh wuh,
sgwan-ngwan dzúh tzáyh.
Khúks saws tu tsáyh,
bús ngok tu náyh!

Gu lhouyh liw-liw,
kwóts tzup skong tou.
Kráys ngan thout you
zuh sah ngáyh ou.

Bamboo Rods

Slender are the bamboo rods
they use for fishing in the Gu.
How can I not think about you?
– But there is no reaching you so far off.

On the left are the springs,
on the right are the waters of Gu.
A lady must journey,
going far away from her family.

On the right are the waters of Gu,
on the left are the springs.
The gleam of your intelligent smile!
The richness of your jade netsuke!

The Gu river flows on,
with oars of juniper they are rowing boats of pine.
I harness words to wander abroad
as a way of releasing my grief.

LIX: Wrats

A married woman remembers the sights of the place where she grew up on the banks of the Gu river, and the lover she left behind there. For a lady to "journey" was a conventional way of referring to marriage to a man belonging to another place.

In Europe, junipers are shrubby plants that could not be used for oars, but the Chinese juniper is a tree.

Tzuh tu lháng i,
Ont kwhu tu dangs i;
swin wuh dzeng i,
nu mah mangs i.

Khomp gu kék káh,
Ont kwhu tu gráh;
mah tóung mah rhas,
druks gu gráks wah.

Khomp gu kék pouh,
Ont kwhu tu lóuh;
mah tóung mah rhas,
druks gu gráks dóu.

Ont Hill

You are so reckless,
there on Ont Hill;
it is true that I'm fond of you,
but I don't admire you.

Thump goes the beating of the drum
below Ont Hill;
in season and out,
your egret's feather is waving.

Thump goes the beating of the pot
on the road to Ont Hill;
in season and out,
your egret's-plume stick is waving.

CXXXVI: Drin

Ont Hill was a rich man's partying place. The egret's plumes were waving in a dance.

Tzús lray, tzús kho,
kwuy ngins Wrats gó.
Kho mráh liw-liw,
ngan tits a Dzóu;
láts-pa bát dap,
ngáyh sum tzúk ou.

Kuts pu ngáyh kráy,
pu nú zon pant.
Gis nayh pu tzáng,
ngáyh su pu wants.
Kuts pu ngáyh kráy,
pu nú zon Tzúys.
Gis nayh pu tzáng,
ngáyh su pu prits.

Tuk payh áy kwhu,
ngan shúh gu mráng.
Nrah-tzuh lant gróuy,
ak kák wuh gráng.
Nghah nin wu tu,
tzoungs druys tsah gwang.

Ngáyh gráng gu lah,
búm-búm gu mrúk.
Khongs wa láts próng;
douy in, douy guk?
Láts-pa koun-tzuh,
mah ngáyh wuh wu.
Prák nayh shah ṣu
pu na ngáyh shah tu.

Gallop, Horses

Gallop, horses, hurry, horses,
taking me home to comfort the lord of Wrats.
The horses have come galloping a long, long way,
and I am reaching Dzóu town;
... but your courtier cuts me off across country,
and so my heart is full of grief.

Now you have disapproved of me,
I cannot turn and go back.
I see you as in the wrong,
and my thoughts will not shift from that.
Now you have disapproved of me,
I cannot turn and cross the Tzúys river again.
I see you as in the wrong,
and my thoughts will not cease.

Walking up that slope
I gather the snake's-head lilies.
Womenfolk are kind and loving,
so we all need to go on visits;
but your people of Nghah object to that:
the whole lot of them are childish and silly.

I walk in the fields;
the wheat is growing thick.
I would throw myself on some great State
– but who can I trust? Who can I turn to?
Courtiers and nobles,
it is not I who am blameworthy.
The hundred things you are thinking
will not stand in my way.

LIV: Long

Most songs in this collection were composed by unknown poets, or in some cases they perhaps evolved with no single author. This is an exception. It is attributed to a known historical figure, who was the sister of Prince Moun of Wrats, and wife of Prince Miwk of the small State of Nghah. Wrats was conquered temporarily by Lék barbarians from the north; in 660 B.C. another

Khóuh bán dzúh kráns.
Dak nin tu kwhán!
Dók mits ngás ngan,
wrank lhih pout whan.

Khóuh bán dzúh áy.
Dak nin tu kwháy!
Dók mits ngás káy,
wrank lhih pout kwáy.

Khóuh bán dzúh rouk.
Dak nin tu lrouk!
Dók mits ngás souk,
wrank lhih pout kóuks.

Continued from previous commentary:
Chinese State helped Prince Moun get back into power, and he then ruled from the town of Dzóu. Evidently the Princess was unhappy in her marriage and used her brother's difficulties as an excuse for escape; but her husband sends a courtier to fetch her back. In the song she seems to waver between pretending that she is making an innocent visit to support her brother, and admitting that she has fled an intolerable marriage.

Snake's-head lilies (*Fritillaria*) were believed in China to make a medicine good for dissipating sadness. For a girl to go on a journey, as in the third verse, standardly refers to her getting married; in this context, though, it makes better sense to interpret it as referring to family visits after marriage.

We Attained Ecstasy

We attained ecstasy by the hidden stream.
Oh, the grandeur of the great man!
I go to bed alone and chatter when I wake.
Never, he swears, will he forget me.

We attained ecstasy on the slope.
Oh, the beauty of the great man!
I go to bed alone and sing when I wake.
Never, he swears, will he be unfaithful.

We attained ecstasy on the hilltop.
Oh, the prominence of the great man!
I go to bed alone and live apart when I wake.
Never, he swears, will he tell others of our love.

LVI: Wrats

Or is it she who is giving her word to him? As usual, the grammatical subjects
are left vague.

Núm shan sdóuy-sdóuy,
wung gwá snouy-snouy.
Ráh lóuh wuh lánk,
Atsúy tzuh lou kwuy.
Kuts wat kwuy tuh,
akát wus gróuy tuh?

Kát kros ngáh brank,
kón nouy shong tuh.
Ráh lóuh wuh lánk,
Atsúy tzuh long tuh.
Kuts wat long tuh,
akát wus dzong tuh?

Ngets mráy na tu gáy?
Gwráng tzong gu móh.
Tsos tsúy na tu gáy?
Pit kóuks bah múh.
Kuts wat kóuks tuh,
akát wus kouk tuh?

Sék sin na tu gáy?
Puyh pah pu khúk.
Tsos tsúy na tu gáy?
Puyh mú pu túk.
Kuts wat túk tuh,
akát wus guk tuh?

The Southern Mountain

The Southern Mountain is high and craggy;
the dog-fox walks slyly.
The road to Ráh is smooth,
and the lady of Atsúy followed it to her new home.
Since we know she has gone,
why are you still yearning for her?

Five pairs of bean-fibre sandals,
and a couple of cap-tassels.
The road to Ráh is smooth,
and the lady of Atsúy took it.
Since we know she has taken it,
why are you still hanging about after her?

How is hemp sown?
You plough your acre longways and crossways.
How does one take a wife?
You must make an announcement to the parents.
Since we know the announcement is made,
why are you still sending your addresses?

How is firewood split?
Without an axe it can't be done.
How does one take a wife?
Without a go-between it is not possible.
Since we know he had one,
why are you still so distraught?

CI: Atsúy

A young man of Atsúy is hankering after a girl who has left to marry a man from Ráh, to the south. (Mt T'ai, the great mountain of eastern China, lies between the two States; the sly fox may represent the outsider who has won the girl.) The man from Ráh has married her fair and square, presenting her father with the bridegroom's traditional gifts of sandals and cap-tassels – which symbolize marriage, since they come in pairs.

Tóng pang tu nit i:
payh tho tah tzuh
dzúh ngáyh stit i.
Dzúh ngáyh stit i!
Rih ngáyh tzit i.

Tóng pang tu ngwat i:
payh tho tah tzuh
dzúh ngáyh lhát i.
Dzúh ngáyh lhát i!
Rih ngáyh pát i.

The Sun in the East

The sun in the east:
that gentle lady
is in my room.
She is in my room!
Stepping towards me, she approaches.

The moon in the east:
that gentle lady
is at my door.
She is at my door!
Stepping past me, she leaves.

XCIX: Atsúy

Why does she visit in the daytime? Because she is married?

Sewh noung dzant hiw,
ngáh mók rang trou;
you wrén hap kho,
oum lins awk zlok,
moun in lrhangs kók.
Kráys ngáyh gu toks.

Ngan níms koun-tzuh,
óun gu na ngok
dzúh gu pránt ók.
Róns ngáyh sum khok.

Sits mouh khónk bouh,
rouk pris dzúh nhouh.
Gu rou deh kloung,

kwá re deh shóum.

Rong dount tu góp,
awk zuh kwét nóup.
Ngan níms koun-tzuh,
óun gu dzúh oup.
Pang gáy way gru,
gá-nan ngáyh níms tu.

Dzant sits khónk goun,
grou-mrou awk dóuys;
móng bat wuh wount,
háh trhangs rós ung,
kráw trhangs nuys kwung,
trouk prits kóunt lúng.
Ngan níms koun-tzuh,
tzúks tsimp tzúks hung;
am-am rang nin,
lrit-lrit túk um.

The Small War-Chariot

The small war-chariot has a low crossboard.
The shafts have five ornamental leather bands;
there are slip-rings and side-leathers,
dark trace-straps with silvered connecting rings,
patterned mats, and protruding wheel-hubs.
He has yoked our black-mottled grey and our horse with a white
 nearside hind leg.
I am thinking of my lord,
how he is polished as jade
amid their wooden huts.
He disturbs the cockles of my heart.

Four stallions, big and heavy,
six reins in hand.
The black-mottled grey and the black-maned bay, they are on the
 inside;
the black-mouthed yellow and the black horse, they are on the
 outside.
The dragon shields overlap one another.
The outside horses' inner reins are buckled with silvered bronze.
I am thinking of my lord,
how polished he is among those country villages:
How long will it be?
How I am thinking of him!

The team of four unmailed horses is well-matched.
The triangular-bladed lances have silvered caps to their shaft-ends.
The covered shields are heavily ornamented.
There are tigerskin bow-cases and engraved breastplates;
two bows are crossed in the bow-cases,
with bamboo rods tied to them to hold their curves.
I am thinking of my lord,
when I lie down and when I awake:
that tranquil, good man –
pure is his reputation.

CXXVIII: Dzin

Commentary overleaf...

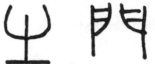

Tóng mún tu lray
kháyh zuh ós mráy.
Payh mruyh Stiwk Ku,
kháyh lah ngás káy.

Tóng mún tu lray
kháyh zuh ós drah.
Payh mruyh Stiwk Ku,
kháyh lah ngás ngah.

Tóng mún tu lray
kháyh zuh ós krán.
Payh mruyh Stiwk Ku,
kháyh lah ngás ngan.

Commentary on previous poem:
The man has gone to war, leaving his lady to yearn for his return; she consoles herself by musing on the dashing figure he cuts among the simple peasantry where he is campaigning. The poem earns its inclusion through the splendid piling up of lovingly-remembered details of the horses and their accoutrements. (Side-leathers were fixed between the horses of a team to prevent them tripping one another.)

88

The Pond by the East Gate

The pond by the East Gate
is used for soaking hemp.
That lovely Third-Daughter Ku,
I could sing to her face to face.

The pond by the East Gate
is used for soaking ramie.
That lovely Third-Daughter Ku,
I could speak to her face to face.

The pond by the East Gate
is used for soaking red-grass.
That lovely Third-Daughter Ku,
I could chat with her face to face.

CXXXIX: Drin

If the girls come to the pool to work, a lad might get his chance to make the acquaintance of one he has noticed. Ramie is a nettle-like Eastern plant equivalent to flax: its fibres are woven into grasscloth. Red-grass (in Australia called kangaroo grass) is a colourful, tough grass species that was used to make mats and ropes.

Kránt i, kránt i!
Pang tzang mrans-mrah,
nit tu pang kloung;
dzúh dzén dangs khah.

Dak nin ngwah-ngwah,
kóng léng mrans-mrah.
Wuh ruk na háh;
tip pris na tzáh.

Tzáyh nhouh tip lewk,
wuh nhouh prank léwk;
hrák na rók tah.
Kóng ngan slék tzewk.

Shan wuh jin,
zup wuh ríng.
Wun douy tu su?
Súy pang mruyh nin.
Payh mruyh nin i,
súy pang tu nin i.

The Scorpion Dance

Oh, so nonchalant!
They are just going to dance the scorpion dance
– the sun is just at its zenith.
He takes the leading place in the front rank.

The great man is tall,
dancing the scorpion dance in the royal courtyard.
He has strength like a tiger;
he grasps reins as if they were mere strings.

In his left hand he holds a flute,
in his right hand he brandishes pheasant feathers.
He gleams red as if freshly-painted.
The prince announces a noble title for him.

On the hill there are hazels,
in the wet ground there are cockleburs.
Pray, who am I thinking about?
The handsome man of the West.
That handsome man,
he is a man from the West!

XXXVIII: Púks

The scorpion dance was a ritual war dance involving battleaxes and shields.

The word *tzewk* refers both to a title of nobility, and to one of the types of ritual bronze vessel that are characteristic artefacts of the Chou dynasty. A *tzewk* (in Mandarin, *chüeh*) was a three-legged wine container with two mushroom-shaped posts rising from the rim. This is not a matter of two words happening to sound alike; just as the Queen makes men knights by tapping them on the shoulder with a sword, so it seems that a Chou prince made someone noble by presenting him with a bronze wine-vessel. Various translators render this line as "ordered him to be given a jar of wine", "ordered him to be given a wine-vessel", and "ordered a title of nobility to be bestowed on him", but these are probably not alternatives: all are simultaneously correct.

In the Chou period, the west of China was the rich and powerful area of the country.

Lah wuh sih kroun,
brák mróu próu tu.
Wuh nrah gróuy thoun,
kit ashuh louh tu.

Rum wuh pók-sók,
lah wuh sih rók;
brák mróu dóun nhok.
Wuh nrah na ngok.

Lha nu lhóts-lhóts i,
mah kómp ngáyh lhots i,
mah shuh mróng lay bots!

A Dead Deer in the Fields

There is a dead fallow-deer in the fields,
wrap it in white cogon grass.
There is a girl full of springtime yearnings,
lucky man, seduce her!

There is undergrowth in the forest,
there is a dead sika-deer in the fields;
tie it into a bundle with white cogon grass.
There is a girl like jade!

Nice and slowly, now!
Don't flutter my neckerchief!
Don't let the dog bark!

XXIII: south of Daws

A hunter is talking to himself: he has brought two deer down and is comparing the task of enticing an attractive girl to the task of dealing with the next deer – both are all too easily frightened away.

Cogon grass is a long reedy type of grass with silky white plumes, widely used in modern times as a packing material.

93

Thout gu tóng mún,
wuh nrah na wun.
Souy tzúk na wun,
puyh ngáyh su dzún.
Káwh uy gu krun,
ríw gráwk ngáyh wun.

Thout gu in tá,
wuh nrah na lá.
Souy tzúk na lá,
puyh ngáyh su dzá.
Káwh uy na-ra,
ríw kháyh lah ngwa.

As I Go Out by the East Gate

As I go out by the East Gate,
there are girls as thickly-packed as clouds.
Although they are like clouds,
it is not them my mind is on.
Plain silk dress and black-mottled grey headcloth:
she will make me happy!

As I go out by the barbican,
there are girls as crowded as dandelions.
Although they are like dandelions,
it is not them my mind turns to.
Plain silk dress and crimson sash:
I can be joyful with her!

XCIII: Dengs

Na-ra in the last but one line means the madder plant, which gives a crimson
dye; according to the commentators, it was understood that the crimson
garment was a sash. The clothes described are those of a poor girl.

Toung poum tsah báwks.
Kás ngáyh tzúk saws,
nghawk rángs saws ngáws.
Kloung sum deh dáwks.

Toung poum tsah mrú.
Wéts-nan khúnk rú,
mák wank mák rú.
Liw-liw ngáyh su.

Toung poum tsah íts.
Pu nit wuh íts,
ngás ngan pu mits.
Kás ngan tzúk títs.

Íts-íts gu oum,
houyh-houyh gu róuy.
Ngás ngan pu mits,
kás ngan tzúk gróuy.

Ceaseless Wind

Ceaseless wind and cloudbursts.
When you look at me, you smile,
but your joking goes too far, your laughter is arrogant.
In my heart, I am sad.

Ceaseless wind and duststorms.
Sweetly, you agree to come to me,
but there is no coming and going.
Longingly I think of you.

Ceaseless wind and overcast skies,
no sun: it is truly overcast.
I go to bed but I cannot sleep;
when I look at you, I feel chagrin.

Oh, the gloominess of the clouds;
the rumbling of the thunder!
I go to bed but I cannot sleep;
when I look at you, I yearn.

XXX: Púks

Wán-rán tu ke,
dóng-tzuh bús whe!
Souy tzúk bús whe,
nú pu ngáyh tre?

Yong i, zouts i,
doy táts gwits i!

Wán-rán tu lap,
dóng-tzuh bús lhap!
Souy tzúk bús lhap,
nú pu ngáyh gráp?

Yong i, zouts i,
doy táts gwits i!

The Rough-Potato Plant

Oh, the branches of the rough-potato plant!
My boy is wearing a marlinspike at his sash!
Even though he is wearing a marlinspike,
can he fail to know me?

Oh, the ceremonial dagger! The jade emblem!
Oh, the trembling of his sash-ends!

Oh, the leaves of the rough-potato plant!
My boy is wearing an archer's thimble at his sash!
Even though he is wearing an archer's thimble,
can he fail to recognize me?

Oh, the ceremonial dagger! The jade emblem!
Oh, the trembling of his sash-ends!

LX: Wrats

A boy has become a man, wearing the accoutrements of adult manhood. (A *whe* was a spike of bone or horn used to undo knots. A *lhap* protected an archer's finger from bowstring burns.) This young man's girl is afraid that he has now become too important to bother with her.

We have seen that many of these poems begin with a scene-setting line that seems disconnected from what follows. This case is extreme. The rough-potato plant (scientifically, *Metaplexis*) is a creeper with showy leaves and flowers; the stalks are edible, and contain a white juice (like milk). One commentator suggests that the singer is contrasting the lad's present appearance of manhood with his having only recently been a milk-drinking child. Perhaps; but one might need to be a Chinese of the first millennium B.C. to be sure of understanding the metaphor.

Kék káh gu tháng,
lonk lawk longs prang.
Lháh kwúk deng Dzóu,
ngáyh dók núm gráng.

Dzong Sóun Tzuh-Gloungs
breng Drin lah Sóungs.

... Pu ngáyh zuh kwuy,
ou sum wuh klhoung.

Wan kra wan khah,
wan smángs gu mráh;
wa zuh grou tu,
wa rum tu gráh.

Sih sheng khét-khót.
Lah tzuh deng lot,
tip tzuh tu nhouh;
lah tzuh krí-róuh.

Wha-tzay, khót i,
pu ngáyh gwát i.
Wha-tzay, whín i,
pu ngáyh nhin i.

100

The Drumbeat

He:
Hark, the boom of the beating drum.
Men are jumping to and brandishing weapons.
They are fortifying the State with earthworks and walling Dzóu
 town;
we alone march south!

Our leader is Sóun Tzuh-Gloungs;
we march to bring peace to the States of Drin and Sóungs.

... But he will not be returning with us;
we are sad at heart and very grieved.

And now we stop, and again we halt;
and now we have lost the horses.
We go searching for them,
down in the forests.

She:
Whether dead or alive, we are far apart.
With you, I was perfectly happy;
I held your hand.
Together with you I was going to grow old.

Alas, separation!
You do not support me.
Alas, distance!
You do not go on with me.

XXXI: Púks

Tzuh tu prhong i!
Zhuh ngáyh á gróngs i:
mhúh la pu sóngs i.

Tzuh tu thang i!
Zhuh ngáyh á dáng i:
mhúh la pu tzang i.

Uy krump kwhenk uy,
dang krump kwhenk dang.
Stiwk i, prák i,
kráys la lah gráng!

Dang krump kwhenk dang,
uy krump kwhenk uy.
Stiwk i, prák i,
kráys la lah kwuy!

If Only

How handsome you are!
You waited for me in the lane:
if only I had walked with you.

How splendid you are!
You waited for me in the hall:
if only I had gone to you.

My top will be brocaded silk with an unlined hemp jacket,
my skirt will be brocaded silk with an unlined hemp overskirt.
Younger brother, elder brother,
yoke me to him so we go away together!

My skirt will be brocaded silk with an unlined hemp overskirt,
my top will be brocaded silk with an unlined hemp jacket.
Younger brother, elder brother,
yoke me to him so we return to his home!

LXXXVIII: Dengs

She hopes, perhaps fantasizes, that it may not be too late for the men of her
family to arrange the marriage.

Payh lrák tu pay
wuh bá lah gáy,
wuh mruyh it nin:
lhang na tu gáy.
Ngás mits mah way,
thíh spits pháng láy.

Payh lrák tu pay
wuh bá lah krén,
wuh mruyh it nin:
dak láts tsah gwren.
Ngás mits mah way,
kloung sum wen-wen.

Payh lrák tu pay
wuh bá gómp-lómp,
wuh mruyh it nin:
dak láts tsah ngam.
Ngás mits mah way,
trent-tront buk koump.

On the Edge of the Marsh

On the edge of that marsh
there are reeds and lotuses;
there is a certain lovely person:
how painful it is!
Waking and sleeping I know not what to do,
my tears and snivel flow freely.

On the edge of that marsh
there are reeds and water-lilies;
there is a certain lovely person,
stately and handsome.
Waking and sleeping I know not what to do,
in my inmost heart I grieve.

On the edge of that marsh
there are reeds and lotus-blossoms;
there is a certain lovely person,
stately and majestic.
Waking and sleeping I know not what to do,
lying on my pillow I toss and turn.

CXLV: Drin

Jin lah Wruh,
pang wháns-wháns i.
Ashuh lah nrah,
pang prank krán i.
Nrah wat "Kón á?"
Ashuh wat "Kuts tza."
"Tsah wank kón á?"
"Wruh tu ngwáts,
whín wrha tsah gráwk."
Wi ashuh lah nrah,
ruy gu sang nghawk.
Dzúngs tu zuh dawk-ráwk.

Jin lah Wruh,
rouh gu tseng uh.
Ashuh lah nrah,
un gu leng uh.
Nrah wat "Kón á?"
Ashuh wat "Kuts tza."
"Tsah wank kón á?"
"Wruh tu ngwáts,
whín wrha tsah gráwk."
Wi ashuh lah nrah,
ruy gu tzang nghawk.
Dzúngs tu zuh dawk-ráwk.

Two Rivers

In the rivers Jin and Wruh
just now the water is high.
Men and girls
just now are holding orchids.
A girl says "Shall we have a look?"
The man says "I have!"
"Shall we go and look again?"
"Beyond the Wruh,
the view is wide and pleasant!"
Men and girls,
this is how they tease each other,
and one gives the other a peony.

In the rivers Jin and Wruh
the clear water is running deep.
Men and girls
are there in great crowds.
A girl says "Shall we have a look?"
The man says "I have!"
"Shall we go and look again?"
"Beyond the Wruh,
the view is wide and pleasant!"
Men and girls,
this is how they tease one another,
and one gives the other a peony.

XCV: Dengs

In the State of Dengs there was a flower festival on the third day of the third
month (corresponding in our calendar to a date in April), held at the meeting of
rivers running high with snow melted in the mountains, and intended to banish
ill omens.

Gip móh tu krén i
sáng tah akrén-akrén i.
Gráng lah tzuh aswen i.

Gip móh tu ngwáts i
sáng tah lats-lats i.
Gráng lah tzuh dats i.

Within the Ten-Acre

Within the ten-acre
the mulberry-leaf pickers are leisurely in their movements.
I'll turn aside with you.

Outside the ten-acre
the mulberry-leaf pickers are slow and spread out.
I'll come away with you.

CXI: Ngwuy

Silkworms live on mulberry leaves, which must be gathered throughout the heat of summer (other harvests wait till summer is turning into autumn). The gatherers are relaxed; no one will notice if two people slip off together.

The Chinese measure land by the *móh*, sometimes called a "Chinese acre". In fact, it is a smaller unit: ten *móh* is about 1½ English acres, but the translation might sound excessively pedantic if it took account of this.

Nrah wat "Ké mreng".
Ashuh wat "Múts táns".
"Tzuh hung gis yaks!"
"Mrang Séng wuh ráns."
"Tsang ngóu tsang zang,
luk bo lah ngráns."

"Luk ngan kráy tu,
lah tzuh ngay tu.
Ngay ngan oump jouh,
lah tzuh krí róuh.
Gum sprit dzúh ngaks,
mák pu dzenk hóuh."

"Tre tzuh tu rú tu,
dzóup bús zuh dzúngs tu.
Tre tzuh tu askouns tu,
dzóup bús zuh mouns tu.
Tre tzuh tu hóus tu,
dzóup bús zuh póus tu.

The Girl Says "The Cock is Crowing"

The girl says "The cock is crowing".
The man says "It's not light yet."
– "Sir, get up and look at the night!"
– "The Morning Star is still bright."
– "Please, stir yourself, please get going,
go and shoot wild duck and wild geese."

"When you have hit one,
I will prepare it for you.
When it is ready, we shall drink wine,
I shall be your companion into old age.
There will be lute and harp when we are served;
everything will be pure and lovely."

– "If I know that you are coming to me,
I will present you with mixed netsuke.
If I know that you will be obedient,
I will sort out some mixed netsuke.
If I know that you love me,
I shall repay you with mixed netsuke."

LXXXII: Dengs

To *luk* was to shoot arrows with strings attached, so the arrow was not lost and the bird, if hit, could easily be retrieved.

陽 陽 辛 同

Koun-tzuh lang-lang.
Tzáyh tip gwáng,
wuh taw ngáyh lou bang.
Gu gráwk teh tza!

Koun-tzuh lou-lou.
Tzáyh tip dóu,
wuh taw ngáyh lou ngáw.
Gu gráwk teh tza!

My Lord is Elated

My lord is elated.
In his left hand he holds his reed-organ,
with his right he beckons me to his room.
Oh, the joy in him!

My lord is pleased with himself.
In his left hand he holds his feather-stick,
with his right he beckons me to the pleasure-land.
Oh, the joy in him!

LXVII: Royal Domain

Tóng mún tu dant,
na-ra dzúh pant.
Gu stit tzúk nuyh,
gu nin goump want.

Tóng mún tu rit,
wuh dzant krá stit.
Khúyh pu nayh sus?
Tzuh pu ngáyh tzit.

By the Sacrifice-Ground

By the sacrifice-ground at the East Gate
madder grows on the bank.
Your home is quite near,
but you yourself are so distant.

The chestnuts at the East Gate
grow among low-fenced houses.
How can I not brood over you?
But you do not come to me.

LXXXIX: Dengs

A *dant* was an area of hard level ground used for offering sacrifices. The
madder and the chestnuts are easy for anyone to gather; likewise the girl is
ready and waiting, if the man would only come.

Dó ngáyh zuh mók-kwrá,
póus tu zuh gweng kra.
Puyh póus lay,
wrank zuh way hóus lay.

Dó ngáyh zuh mók gláw,
póus tu zuh gweng law.
Puyh póus lay,
wrank zuh way hóus lay.

Dó ngáyh zuh mók ruh,
póus tu zuh gweng kwuh.
Puyh póus lay,
wrank zuh way hóus lay.

The Quince

She threw me a quince,
I paid her with a jewel pendant.
It was not payment:
it was to represent my love for ever.

She threw me a peach,
I paid her with a jasper gem.
It was not payment:
it was to represent my love for ever.

She threw me a plum,
I paid her with an obsidian gem.
It was not payment:
it was to represent my love for ever.

LXIV: Wrats

Drou-mliw nhok sin,
Sóum Séng dzúh lhín.
Kum zak gáy zak,
kéns tseyh rang nin.
Tzuh i, tzuh i,
na tseyh rang nin gáy!

Drou-mliw nhok cho,
Sóum Séng dzúh ngo.
Kum zak gáy zak,
kéns tseyh grés-grós.
Tzuh i, tzuh i,
na tseyh grés-grós gáy!

Drou-mliw nhok chah,
Sóum Séng dzúh gáh.
Kum zak gáy zak,
kéns tseyh tsáns tah.
Tzuh i, tzuh i,
na tseyh tsáns tah gáy!

Tied Together

The bundle of firewood is tied together,
the Three Stars are in the sky.
What a night tonight will be,
seeing these lovely women!
Such girls, such girls,
what women are as lovely as these!

The bundle of hay is tied together,
the Three Stars are at the corner.
What a night tonight will be,
seeing this carefree happiness!
Such girls, such girls,
what happiness is as carefree as this!

The bundle of brushwood is tied together,
the Three Stars are at the door.
What a night tonight will be,
seeing this beauty-threesome!
Such girls, such girls,
what three are as beautiful as this!

CXVIII: Gláng

When a man of rank married, he was given not only the girl he requested as
principal wife, but also a suitable number (depending on his status) of her
female relatives, as concubines. This man rates one-plus-two, who are now tied
to him in marriage as a bundle of sticks is tied with cord. He compares them
with the constellation of Three Stars, also known as the Heart. The Chinese
divide up the zodiac differently from Europeans, grouping its stars into 28
rather than twelve constellations: the Heart comprises the bright star Antares
and two lesser stars in our constellation of Scorpio.

Whéts pay sewh séng,
Sóum Ngáh dzúh tóng.
Siwk-siwk sew teng
souk yaks dzúh kóng.
Dúk mring pu dóng.

Whéts pay sewh séng,
wi Lhum lah Mróuh.
Siwk-siwk sew teng,
bóuh khum lah drou.
Dúk mring pu you.

Little Stars

Those little stars are twinkling,
the Three and the Five in the east.
We scurry off on our night-expeditions
at the Palace in the early hours.
Truly, our fate is not the same as hers.

Those little stars are twinkling,
only Orion's Belt and the Pleiades are left.
We scurry away on our night-expeditions
carrying quilt and nightdress in our arms.
Truly, our fate is not like hers.

XXI: south of Daws

For lesser wives or concubines, life was not always so carefree. Here, they compare their lot with the principal wife, who lives in the fine rooms of the Palace by day as well as night. They, by contrast, visit the master when he summons them at night and then hasten back to the women's quarters in the small hours.

Sóum Ngáh, the Three and the Five, are constellations; the Three or Heart was mentioned in "Tied Together", but I do not know which European constellation the Five corresponds to.

Sin lú wuh tseyh,
gáy lhouyh meyh-meyh.
Ént-ont tu grou:
gak-la pu sent.

Sin lú wuh súyh,
gáy lhouyh múyh-múyh.
Ént-ont tu grou:
gak-la pu dúnt.

Nga mank tu lhet,
góng tzúk tu ray.
Ént-ont tu grou:
túk tseyh tsou-lhay.

The New Tower

The New Tower is brightly decorated,
and the waters of the river are deep and clear.
She had looked for someone handsome:
this mat-roll of a man is nothing special.

The New Tower is freshly cleaned,
and the waters of the river are flowing smoothly.
She had looked for someone handsome:
this mat-roll of a man is no good.

She set up her fish-net,
but it trapped a goose.
She had looked for someone handsome:
she got this toad!

XLIII: Púks

The New Tower looks promising as the home of a good match, but the man who lives there is a disappointment. A *gak-la* is a rough bamboo mat; it would often be kept rolled up, in which case it is seen as resembling a stiff, clumsy man.

Prák i krhat i,
próng tu grat i!
Prák lay tip do,
way wang dzén kho.

Dzus prák tu tóng,
lhouh na puy bóng.
Khúyh mah káws mók,
douy drék way yong?

Gu wah, gu wah!
Kóuh-kóuh thout nit.
Ngons ngan su prák,
kám sum lhouh dzit.

En túk whan tsóuh?
Ngan dos tu púks.
Ngons ngan su prák,
shuh ngáyh sum múks.

My Warlike Lord

How warlike my lord appears!
He is the hero of the nation.
My lord grasps his lance,
he rides in the king's vanguard.

Since my lord rode east
my hair has been like mugwort flying in the wind.
Of course I have lotions and shampoos,
but who cares to put effort into appearance?

How it rains, how it rains!
Let the sun shine out brightly.
Longingly I think of my lord,
there is sweetness in my heart but my head aches.

How can I get the herb of forgetfulness?
I would plant it at the back of the house.
Longingly I think of my lord,
it makes my heart distressed.

LXII: Wrats

Mugwort is a common weed in England; no woman would be flattered to have
her hair likened to it, but it does not look *more* obviously untidy than many
other plants. However, in Old Chinese there happened to be another word,
also pronounced *bóng*, which meant "disorderly", so perhaps this coincidence
of sounds led the Chinese to think of mugwort as the untidy weed *par
excellence*, as we think of the lion as the supremely brave animal, whether it is
truly braver than others or not.

The herb of forgetfulness was said to be a plant that one could cook,
flowers and leaves together, to make a potion that led to forgetting one's
sorrows. Probably the species was mythical, though some have identified it
with one of the shade-loving hostas. The rear of the house is where the
women's quarters are, so the herb would be handy for use.

Kram-krá sháng-sháng,
brák gráks way shang.
Shah wuts "ruy nin"
dzúh lhouyh it pang.
Sngáks wúy dzong tu,
lóuh jah tsah atrang.
Sngáks you dzong tu,
ont dzúh lhouyh kloung ang.

Kram-krá tsúy-tsúy,
brák gráks mouts huy.
Shah wuts "ruy nin"
dzúh lhouyh tu mruy.
Sngáks wúy dzong tu,
lóuh jah tsah tzúy.
Sngáks you dzong tu,
ont dzúh lhouyh kloung druy.

Kram-krá shúh-shúh,
brák gráks mouts luh.
Shah wuts "ruy nin"
dzúh lhouyh tu zhuh.
Sngáks wúy dzong tu,
lóuh jah tsah wuh.
Sngáks you dzong tu,
ont dzúh lhouyh kloung tuh.

Reeds

The reeds are green,
the white dew is turning to frost.
He I call "the one and only"
is somewhere about the river.
I go after him upstream;
the way is difficult and long.
I go after him downstream;
he eludes me in the middle of the river.

The reeds are dense,
the white dew has not yet been dried by the sun.
He I call "the one and only"
is on the margin of the river.
I go after him upstream;
the way is difficult and steep.
I go after him downstream;
he eludes me among the islets in the stream.

The reeds are full of colour,
the white dew is not yet finished.
He I call "the one and only"
is on the bank of the river.
I go after him upstream;
the way is difficult and winding.
I go after him downstream;
he eludes me among the eyots in the river.

CXXIX: Dzin

A girl hopes to encounter a man whose name she is perhaps too shy to utter.
Struggling along the rough tracks through the river area where he is working,
she fails to catch him up – because he is avoiding her, or because he is unaware
of her presence? We do not know.

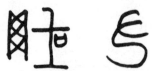

Kwruh wruk tu nga:
dzóunt bang.
Ngáyh kós tu tzuh
kóunt uy siwks dang.

Góng puy tzoun tah.
Kóng kwuy mah shah;
a na nhin khah.

Góng puy tzoun rouk.
Kóng kwuy pu bouk;
a na nhin souk.

Deh zuh wuh kóunt uy i,
mah zuh ngáyh kóng kwuy i,
mah shuh ngáyh sum pruy i!

The Netted Fish

The fish in the nine nets
are salmon and bream.
You, when we met,
wore a royal dragon coat and an embroidered robe.

The wild goose flies along the island.
When the prince goes home, there will be no place for us there;
I will stay with you one more night.

The wild goose flies along the scarp.
When the prince goes home, he will not return;
I will sleep with you once more.

So, you of the dragon coat,
don't go back with our prince,
don't make my heart grieve!

CLIX: Prun

Again the poem begins with a scene-setting passage disconnected from the main theme: I do not know the relevance of the salmon and bream. (*Dzóunt* is a Pacific salmon species – Americans call it cherry.) The overall idea is clear: the singer has become involved with a nobleman who arrived in the prince's retinue, but the prince and he are now due to depart.

Prun was a small State, notable as the home of the first Chou emperor.

Lang tu lhouyh
pu rou nhok sin.
Payh gu tu tzuh
pu lah ngáyh stos Nhin.
Gróuy tzú, gróuy tzú!
akát ngwat la aswen kwuy tzú?

Lang tu lhouyh
pu rou nhok chah.
Payh gu tu tzuh
pu lah ngáyh stos Pah.
Gróuy tzú, gróuy tzú!
akát ngwat la aswen kwuy tzú?

Lang tu lhouyh
pu rou nhok bá.
Payh gu tu tzuh
pu lah ngáyh stos Nghah.
Gróuy tzú, gróuy tzú!
akát ngwat la aswen kwuy tzú?

Rising Water

Rising water
will not float apart sticks that are tied together.
That lady there
is not with me guarding the Nhin border.
Oh love, oh love!
What month shall I return home?

Rising water
will not float apart brushwood that is tied together.
That lady there
is not with me guarding the Pah border.
Oh love, oh love!
What month shall I return home?

Rising water
will not float apart reeds that are tied together.
That lady there
is not with me guarding the Nghah border.
Oh love, oh love!
What month shall I return home?

LXVIII: Royal Domain

Although the rising tide of war is keeping the couple apart physically, it cannot break the marriage bond.

Tzuh wéts su ngáyh,
khan dang dap Jin.
Tzuh pu ngáyh su,
khúyh mah lháy nin?
Gwang dóng tu gwang lay tza!

Tzuh wéts su ngáyh,
khan dang dap Wruh.
Tzuh pu ngáyh su,
khúyh mah lháy ashuh?
Gwang dóng tu gwang lay tza!

Tucking Up My Skirt

If you think of me fondly,
I'd tuck up my skirt and wade across the Jin river.
But if you don't think about me,
do you imagine there is no one else out there?
You are the silliest of silly boys!

If you think of me fondly,
I'd tuck up my skirt and wade across the Wruh river.
But if you don't think about me,
do you imagine there are no other men out there?
You are the silliest of silly boys!

LXXXVII: Dengs

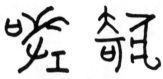

Ay-tzay, thang i!
Guy nu atrang i,
ik nak lang i,
mruyh mouk lang i!
Khúks tso-tsang i;
laks tzúk tzáng i.

Ay-tzay, meng i!
Mruyh mouk tseng i,
ngay kuts deng i.
Toung nit laks gó,
pu thout teng i.
Trent ngáyh sheng i!

Ay-tzay, bront i!
Tseng lang ont i.
Mrah tzúk sont i;
laks tzúk kóns i.
Sits lhih pant i,
zuh ngrah róns i!

134

Ay-tzay!

Ay-tzay! How splendid!
He is tall and long-legged.
Oh, such a forehead:
beautiful eyes and forehead!
Nimble is his footwork;
when he shoots he is skilled.

Ay-tzay! How illustrious!
His beautiful eyes are clear;
his manners are already perfect.
All day he shoots at the target,
and never misses the bullseye.
He is a true nephew of mine!

Ay-tzay! How handsome!
His clear forehead is gentle.
Dancing, he keeps time;
shooting, he pierces the centre of the target.
His flight of four arrows each find their way to it:
he could put down a rebellion!

CVI: Atsúy

Archery contests were rituals that involved dancing as well as shooting; the archers may have been required to co-ordinate their shots with steps of a fixed dance, making for a greater challenge than shooting from a standing position. The target would have been painted on a hanging cloth or hide, and "piercing the centre" might imply not just hitting the right spot but with sufficient force to go through.

Pride in a fine young kinsman is one kind of love. But my main reason for including this, being myself a shooter whose rounds all too often stray from the mark, and a dancer whose feet have been known to lose the rhythm, is that I just love this song. *Ay-tzay!*

Shan wuh ba-sngá,
zup wuh gáy wrhá.
Pu kéns tzuh Tá,
nuh kéns gwang tza.

Shan wuh akaw skong,
zup wuh you rong.
Pu kéns tzuh Thong,
nuh kéns kráwh dóng.

Odd Encounters

On the hill are *ba-sngá* trees,
in the boggy ground are lotus flowers.
I don't encounter Mr Tá,
I just encounter a daftie.

On the hill are tall pines,
in the boggy ground are wandering-dragons.
I don't encounter Mr Thong,
I just encounter a weird boy.

LXXXIV: Dengs

Not enough Mr Rights and too many losers are a problem for single girls down the ages.

It is not certain what kind of tree a *ba-sngá* was; one dictionary thinks this is an alternative to *sáng* as a name for the mulberry. Wandering-dragons were a plant (*Polygonum orientale*) with sprays of red flowers which nod in the breeze; Americans call it Kiss-me-over-the-garden-gate.

Gráng mún tu gráh
kháyh zuh súy-druy;
prits tu yang-yang
kháyh zuh raws kruy.

Khúyh gu luk nga
pit Gáy tu bang?
Khúyh gu tsos tsúy
pit Atsúy tu Kang?

Khúyh gu luk nga
pit Gáy tu ruh?
Khúyh gu tsos tsúy
pit Sóungs tu Tzuh?

If One Eats a Fish

Beneath my rustic lintel
I can feel at ease.
The bubbling of the spring
will assuage my hunger pangs.

If one eats a fish,
why should it have to be a Yellow River bream?
If one takes a wife,
why should she have to be a Kang of Atsúy?

If one eats a fish,
why should it have to be a Yellow River carp?
If one takes a wife,
why should she have to be a Tzuh of Sóungs?

CXXXVIII: Drin

Bream and carp from the Yellow River were specially prized by gourmets; the Kangs of Atsúy and the Tzuhs of Sóungs were distinguished families. The singer is resisting pressure to make a "good marriage".

The opening word, *gráng*, means a horizontal crossbeam; the commentators tell us that a *gráng mún*, literally a "crossbeam-doorway", implied a doorway formed from a treetrunk as lintel – hence the doorway of a simple rustic home.

139

Máw kwhu tu kát i,
gáy dánt tu tzík i!
Stiwk i, prák i,
gáy táy nit lay?
Gáy gu khah lay?
Pit wuh lah lay.
Gáy gu kwuh lay?
Pit wuh zuh lay.

Gwá gwu móng-nong.
Puyh ka pu tóng,
stiwk i, prák i,
mayh shah lah dóng.
Sáyh i, muyh i,
rou-ray tu tzuh!
Stiwk i, prák i,
zous na thong nuh.

The lablab bean is both a food source and a showily ornamental plant, with pink flowers and purple pods on vines up to thirty feet long. But, as often, the opening lines have limited relevance to the main theme. If Máw is the proper name of a hill, we do not know where it was; the commentators claim that it is a descriptive word ("backward-sloping"), but, either way, we cannot now recover the connexion of ideas between the beans on the hill and the girl's frantic appeals to the menfolk of her family. The "brothers" may be the singer's own brothers, or her uncles – that is, her father's elder and younger brothers. In either case, they would be suitable escorts for her, if willing: but it sounds as though they are not disposed to help, and a girl certainly could not go travelling on her own.

It must be said that, while some lines here seem very understandable, other parts remain fairly mysterious. Why does the singer suddenly break off to comment on the owl chicks? – can this be intended to suggest a charming butterfly mind, or does that read 21st-century judgements into a first-

The Lablab Beans

The lablab beans on Máw Hill,
how rampantly their vines spread!
Younger brother, elder brother,
how many days will he be?
Where is he staying?
He must have someone with him.
How much longer will he be?
He must be up to something.

The foxfur coats are shaggy.
It isn't that carriages are not travelling east,
younger brother, elder brother,
only there is no one for me to travel with.
– Oh, how tiny, how cute,
the owl chicks!
Younger brother, elder brother,
in full dress, as if your ears were stopped!

XXXVII: Púks

millennium-B.C. world where they are alien? We know that *muyh* is a variant of the normal pronunciation *mruyh* for "beautiful", so the baby-talk connotations of "cute" are perhaps suitable. But if my translation of that line is defensible, my treatment of the last line is probably less so. *Thong nuh* is literally "to fill the ear(s)", and it commonly refers to the ornamental earplugs which, we have seen, were a significant component of Chou-dynasty formal dress, though we do not know what they looked like or what their purpose was. Most translators take the last line to be a pettish comment on the fact that the brothers are stolidly standing by in full dress, with sleeved coats and earplugs, while the girl wants action. But the grammar seems slightly odd if that is the meaning, so I wonder whether *na* should be read as "as" rather than "you" (it can mean either), and the girl is accusing them of behaving as though they could not hear her.

Lah wuh mans tsóuh,
ríng gráks dón i.
Wuh mruyh it nin,
tseng lang ont i.
Grés-grós sang ngos,
stek ngáyh ngons i.

Lah wuh mans tsóuh,
ríng gráks nang-nang.
Wuh mruyh it nin,
ont na tseng lang.
Grés-grós sang ngos,
lah tzuh krí tzáng.

Dew on the Creepers

The fields are covered with creepers,
the falling dew is heavy.
Here is a certain lovely person;
her clear forehead is beautiful.
In carefree mood we happen to meet,
and she falls in with my desire.

The fields are covered with creepers,
the falling dew is thick.
Here is a certain lovely person;
beautiful is your clear forehead.
In carefree mood we happen to meet;
you and I are good together.

XCIV: Dengs

Some scholars would say that I am reading too much into the sixth line; as normal, there is no subject, and *stek ngáyh ngons* could merely mean that the chance encounter in itself was what the singer had yearned for. According to Bernhard Karlgren, it is not even clear whether the "lovely person" is a woman rather than a handsome man. And he takes the closing phrase *krí tzáng* to be a variation on the standard formula *krí róuh*, "grow old together", making the last line not a statement but a marriage proposal.

This seems to stretch the normal meaning of *tzáng*, though. Ambiguity is inseparable from Chinese poetry; that admitted, on balance my interpretation seems the most straightforward and best bet.

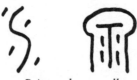

Prits payh sgwan lhouyh
ak rou wa Gu.
Wuh gróuy wa Wrats:
mayh nit pu su.
Bront payh ta Ku,
rív lah tu mu.

Thout souk wa Tzíh,
oump dzans wa Níh.
Nrah-tzuh wuh gráng,
wants bah wrhang díh.
Mouns ngáyh ta ká,
zouts gup prák tzih.

Thout souk wa Kán,
oump dzans wa Ngan.
Tzúks ki, tzúks grát,
aswen ka ngan mráts.
Don djin wa Wrats,
pu grá wuh akáts.

Ngáyh su Buy Sgwan,
tzu tu wrank nhán.
Su So lah Dzóu;
ngáyh sum liw-liw!

Spring Water

The water bubbling up in this very spring,
will flow into the river Gu.
I have a love in the State of Wrats:
not a day but I think about him.
The Ku's are lovely people,
I must involve them in the planning.

If we make the first overnight stop at Tzíh,
we can hold the farewell party at Níh.
A lady has to make her journey,
going far away from father and brothers.
I must get advice from my aunts,
and my girl-cousins, too.

Or if we stop overnight at Kán,
we can hold the farewell party at Ngan.
Then comes the axle-grease! Then comes servicing the linchpins!
There, the returning carriages will leave us.
If we are in too much of a rush to reach Wrats,
there is sure to be a breakdown.

I am thinking about Fat Spring,
I am for ever sighing for that place.
I am thinking about So and Dzóu towns;
my heart longs!

XXXIX: Púks

The natural aim for love is marriage, and planning wedding details is a perennially absorbing feminine activity. This singer, from the small hill State of Púks, is to marry a man from the much larger State of Wrats, on the river Gu downstream.

In China, a groom did not fetch his bride: he (or his parents) sent for her. But when someone went on a journey, the done thing in China was to accompany the traveller for the first stretch. Consequently, the *dzans* feast associated with a marriage was not a "reception", where the bride's parents welcomed the groom and his family to their home, but a party on the road to bid the bride farewell. (We cannot now identify most of the locations mentioned here, which were not necessarily large places even in Chou-dynasty terms.)

A traveller was escorted only for a fraction of the trip. The main part of the journey began once the escort had turned back: so that was the time for fettling the vehicles to face the rigours of the road.

The Introduction mentioned that I have made occasional textual emendations. By far the largest is here: I have omitted the last two lines of the received text completely. They are identical to the last lines of "Bamboo Rods" (pp. 74–5); the themes of the poems are different, but evidently the composer of one borrowed elements from the other. (Both also include the awkward five-syllable line listing family members, discussed in the Introduction; to preserve the rhyme scheme, in this case I treat "mother" as the non-original interpolation.) It is surely "Spring Water" which borrowed from "Bamboo Rods", not the other way round. The closing couplet is integral to the theme of "Bamboo Rods", but (however one translates it) it seems redundant and "tacked on" here.

Thus, rather than concluding "Spring Water", and this book, on the word *ou*, grief, I prefer to end with *liw*, longing: a more plausible emotion for a loving girl impatient for marriage.

APPENDIX:
SPELLING SYSTEMS FOR OLD CHINESE

The Old Chinese spelling system used in this book is based on that of William H. Baxter's 1992 *Handbook of Old Chinese Phonology*, but with adaptations to make it suitable for a general readership.

The principles followed in these adaptations were twofold. On the one hand, I assume that Baxter's reconstruction of Old Chinese pronunciation is essentially correct, and my spelling represents all the phonetic distinctions he identifies – limitations of the Roman alphabet are not allowed to justify writing separate Old Chinese sounds as though they were the same (except in a few marginal cases where Baxter himself expresses doubt about the reconstruction). On the other hand, the spellings should look as natural as possible to readers accustomed to English spelling conventions; Old Chinese should not just be pronounceable but look pronounceable.

This means in the first place that there should be no special phonetic symbols and, ideally, no accented letters. These things are indispensable in scientific linguistic studies (though Baxter makes less use of them than many scholars in this field), but they are very offputting to the general reader whose interests are literary and aesthetic rather than scientific. My spelling scheme uses 22 of the 26 letters of our alphabet (several letters, such as *f* and *v*, are no use for spelling Old Chinese); the only departure from the ideal is that it also uses the acute accent, which is a familiar symbol to English speakers.

Furthermore, so far as possible the letters are used in normal-looking patterns. For instance, Baxter follows the International Phonetic Alphabet in using the letter *x* for the sound in Scottish "loch"; but words beginning with *x* look very queer to English eyes, so I use *h* for this purpose. Likewise, I change Baxter's *hw*, *hl*, *hm*, etc. to *wh*, *lh*, *mh*, etc. because this fits the pattern of English letter-combinations better.

Since Baxter's barred-i symbol is not available for the high back spread vowel, I use *u* for that sound, and write *ou* for Baxter's *u*. The glottal stop in combination with m, n, and ng is written *mp*, *nt*, *nk*; after a vowel it is written as *h*, since this is the only alphabetic letter that looks acceptable to English-speakers to represent a throat sound which is not distinctive enough to interfere with rhyming. (In practice I imagine that most readers who say the poems out loud will ignore the closing *h* letters.) To avoid letter-sequences which many readers would find odd, I write Baxter's *sr zr tsr tshr dzr* as *sh zh j ch dj* respectively. (If this seems to distort Baxter's reconstruction, one can regard my spellings as arbitrary codes for his sequences; but, while Old Chinese *sr* surely was phonemically a cluster, phonetically it could already have been the simple retroflex fricative of modern Mandarin.) Then Baxter's contrast between *tsh* and *ts*, when not followed by *r*, becomes *ts* versus *tz*.

There are special problems about the letter *j* in Baxter's system. Following the International Phonetic Alphabet, *j* is used for the semivowel written *y* in English, as in yacht or yellow. This sound is peculiarly frequent in Old Chinese as reconstructed by Baxter. *J* appears in strange combinations with preceding consonants, and the language seems to prefer diphthongs in *j-*, and even triphthongs in *j...j*, to simple vowels. Baxter is aware of this oddity, though his discussion concludes that the reconstruction is probably nevertheless correct. But even if Baxter's *j* were replaced by *y*, the resulting combinations might look queer to English readers.

Where Baxter writes *j* before a vowel, this represents one hypothesis about the phonetic nature of so-called "Class III finals" – there are other hypotheses in the scholarly literature, for instance it may have been a distinction of vowel length rather than presence versus absence of a semivowel. My spelling finesses this issue by writing an acute accent on non-Class-III syllables, i.e. I put an acute on all those syllables which do *not* have a prevocalic *j* in Baxter's system. In this way, the scientific facts are preserved while leaving those who recite the poems aloud free to ignore an obscure aspect of the pronunciation. Since there is no Old Chinese contrast between *-ij* and *-i*, I omit *-j* from the former. Then remaining cases of Baxter's *j* can be spelled as *y* without an unnatural appearance.

Laurent Sagart (*The Roots of Old Chinese*, 1999), while accepting the general outline of Baxter's reconstructed sound-system, differs from him on the pronunciation of many individual words; in general, I follow Baxter rather than Sagart. (I am agnostic about Sagart's idea that Old Chinese consonant clusters are invariably produced by a rich system of affixation.) I follow Edwin Pulleyblank (*Outline of Classical Chinese Grammar*, p. 103) in assuming that the character for the common negative particle, *bù* in modern Mandarin, was in Old Chinese pronounced *pu* rather than *póut* as implied by the modern forms. (In this Appendix, Mandarin forms are shown in *pinyin* romanization.)

I was strongly tempted to use the letter *q* to represent Baxter's *k*^{w} and *-wk*, which would have avoided the oddity of using alternative letter-combinations for the same single sound, and would also have introduced greater visual distinctiveness among the large range of syllables beginning with *k*. But spellings involving the letter *q* without *u* look strange to English-speakers, which tipped the balance in favour of writing *kw-* and *-wk*.

Baxter uses capitals such as *S* and *N* not for distinct sounds, but as a device to mark cases where reconstructed sounds developed in a non-standard way in the later history of the language. Issues like that are beyond the scope of this book, so I write ordinary lower-case *s*, *n*. Likewise, I ignore the hyphen used by Baxter to distinguish e.g. *b-róng* "well-fed" from *bróng* "huge", since this mark relates to the grammar of the words rather than to their pronunciation. I use hyphens only to link syllables into words.

Baxter reconstructs a voiced *ɦ* at the beginning of certain words. I spell this as *a* when it precedes a consonant, but (following suggestions in a 1983 paper by Pulleyblank), as zero in the unstressed enclitics *uh*, *an*, *á* (Mandarin *yǐ*, *yān*, *hū*), and as *w* in *wóh* "after" (Mandarin *hòu*). I assume also that the consonant in the rhythmic particle *xí* in its modern reading pronunciation is a non-original outgrowth akin to the *h* of *hū* in Pulleyblank's interpretation.

A minor oddity in Baxter's scheme is the voicing contrasts he postulates among initial glides. Each of the glides *j*, *w*, and *r*, when not preceded by another consonant, come (according to Baxter) in three varieties: plain *j*, *w*, *r*; glottalized *ʔj*, *ʔ*^{w}, *ʔr*; and voiceless *hj*, *hw*, *hr*. This seems phonetically implausible, and all the more so since there are no corresponding contrasts among full vowels (no *a-* versus *ʔa-* versus *ha-*, e.g.) – syllables with no other initial consonant always begin with a glottal stop. (Since the Roman alphabet has no letter for the glottal stop and its occurrence in this position is non-contrastive, my spellings omit it.) In the case of *j* Baxter recognizes (p. 203) that this aspect of his reconstruction is questionable; any word reconstructed by Baxter as beginning with *j-* could equally well (so far as we can tell from its later pronunciation) have begun with Baxter's *lj-* or *r-*, and he uses *j-* in essence as a code to indicate that there is no evidence in the writing system pointing towards one rather than the other of the latter alternatives. Likewise Baxter's *hj-* indicates absence of reason to choose among various other sounds which would lead to the same later pronunciation.

These oddities and uncertainties make my choice of spellings rather arbitrary in this area. Since the letter *y* is available for Baxter's *j-*, I use that; and Baxter's *ɟ* initial is adequately represented in my spelling by lack of an acute accent on the following vowel. I spell Baxter's *hj-* words as if he had reconstructed them with one or another of *hlj-*, *hnj-*, or *stj-*; the choice between these is necessarily arbitrary, though Sagart (p. 29) gives reasons for choosing *hnj-* in the word for "hand".

Baxter's *ʔʷ-* and *r-* each occur in only one word found in the poems selected for this volume – the word which Baxter writes *ʔʷjen*, "grieved", and the word for "peony", which in Baxter's spelling would be *djawk-rawk*. Rather than inventing unique spelling conventions for individual words, I spell these words as if Baxter had written them *wjen* and *djawk-ʔrawk*. Baxter's *hw*, *hr* are in my spelling *wh*, *rh*.

Baxter sometimes shows a consonant in brackets, indicating uncertainty about whether the pronunciation did or did not include it, and he writes *C* for a postulated stop consonant of unknown place of articulation. I normally omit these elements (some bracketed letters are retained in order to differentiate separate words).

Since Baxter's book does not include a comprehensive lexicon parallel to Bernhard Karlgren's listing of reconstructed Old Chinese pronunciations, I cannot be sure that I have always correctly understood how Baxter's reworking of Karlgren's system affects particular words. Undoubtedly I will have made some mistakes. But these should not affect the poetic properties of the transcriptions too seriously, because Baxter does explicitly give his versions of all *Stu* rhyme words.

BIBLIOGRAPHY

Barber, Elizabeth W., *The Mummies of Ürümchi*, paperback edition. Pan Books, London, 2000.

Baxter, W. H., *A Handbook of Old Chinese Phonology*. Mouton de Gruyter, Berlin, 1992.

Boltz, W. G., *The Origin and Early Development of the Chinese Writing System*. American Oriental Society, New Haven, Conn., 1994.

Chang Yün-chung, *Pai-hua Chu-chiai Shih Ching*. Commercial Press, Taipei, 60th year of the Republic (= 1971).

Dawson, R., ed., *The Legacy of China*. Clarendon Press, Oxford, 1964.

Empson, W., *Seven Types of Ambiguity*, 3rd edition. Penguin, Harmondsworth, Mddx, 1961.

Grigson, G., *The Englishman's Flora*. Reprinted by Helicon Publishing, Oxford, 1996.

Herrmann, A., *An Historical Atlas of China*, new edition. Edinburgh University Press, 1966.

Hsü Shen, *Shuo Wen Chiai Tzu*. Reprint of the Sung dynasty edition by Hsü Hsüan, Chung-hua Shu-chü, Kowloon, 1972.

Karlgren, B., *Glosses on the Book of Odes. Bulletin of the Museum of Far Eastern Antiquities*, Stockholm, vol. 14, 1942, pp. 71–247, vol. 16, 1944, pp. 25–169, and vol. 18, 1946, pp. 1–198.

Karlgren, B., *The Book of Odes: Chinese Text, Transcription and Translation*. Museum of Far Eastern Antiquities, Stockholm, 1950.

Karlgren, B., *Grammata Serica Recensa. Bulletin of the Museum of Far Eastern Antiquities*, Stockholm, vol. 29, 1957, pp. 1–332.

Karlgren, B., *Sound and Symbol in Chinese*, revised edition. Hong Kong University Press, 1962.

Le Roy Ladurie, E., *Montaillou*, paperback edition. Penguin, Harmondsworth, Mddx, 1980.

Legge, J., *The Chinese Classics*, vol. iv: *The She King*. Reprint of the second edition, Wen Hsing Shu-chü, Taipei, 55th year of the Republic (= 1966).

Liu, J. J. Y., *The Art of Chinese Poetry*. Routledge and Kegan Paul, London, 1962.

Loewe, M., ed., *Early Chinese Texts*. Institute of East Asian Studies, Berkeley, Calif., 1993.

Loewe, M, and Shaughnessy, E. L., eds., *The Cambridge History of Ancient China: From the Origins of Civilization to 221 B.C.* Cambridge University Press, 1999.

Maspero, J., *La Chine antique*, new edition. Imprimerie Nationale, Paris, 1955.

Norman, J., *Chinese*. Cambridge University Press, 1988.

Pulleyblank, E. G., "The locative particles *yu, yu, hu*". *Journal of the American Oriental Society*, vol. 106, 1986, pp. 1–12.

Pulleyblank, E. G., *Outline of Classical Chinese Grammar*. University of British Columbia Press, Vancouver, 1995.

Reischauer, E. O. and Fairbank, J. K., *East Asia: The Great Tradition*. Houghton Mifflin, Boston, Mass., 1960.

Sagart, L., *The Roots of Old Chinese*. John Benjamins, Amsterdam, 1999.

Sampson, G. R., *Brissac and its Mediæval Seigneurs*. Published by www.ruecaterine.com, 2002.

Thurgood, G. and LaPolla, R. J., eds., *The Sino-Tibetan Languages*. Routledge, London, 2003.

Tz'u Hai (2 vols.). Chung-hua Shu-chü, Kunming, 27th year of the Republic (= 1938).

Wheatley, P., *The Pivot of the Four Quarters*. Edinburgh University Press, 1971.

Willetts, W., *Chinese Art* (2 vols.). Penguin, Harmondsworth, Mddx, 1958.

GLOSSARY

The words "a" and "to" are used in this glossary to distinguish noun from verb meanings, for instance "a crow" versus "to crow". But the same Old Chinese word will correspond in context to different grammatical forms of the English gloss: the word glossed "a crow" can equally well mean "(several) crows", the word for "to crow" can translate as "crowing", "crowed", etc.

a, á	at
á	1. a crow
	2. ... *á?* changes statement to question
á-nu	a closing exclamation
ak	but, so
akát	why?, what?, where?, etc.
akáts	to hurt, be hurt
akaw	high
akrén	to move leisurely
akwáng	yellow
am	tranquil
an	... and that's that
ang	the centre
ashuh	a gentleman
askouns	to obey
aswen	to turn round
atrang	long
atraw	a court, a morning reception of visitors
aw	young and lovely
awk	silver, silvered
áwk	rich and glossy
ay-tzay	an exclamation
áy	a slope
ayh-nayh	luxuriant
ba, ba-buk	to crawl
ba-sngá	a kind of tree, possibly mulberry
bá	reeds

bah	father
ban	an uncoloured garment
bán	joy
bang	1. a room
	2. a bream
bat	a shield
bát	to trudge; *bát dap* "trudge and wade": to go across country
báwks	violent, a cloudburst
benk	together
bewh	to drop
bih	to compare
bis	braid
bo	a wild duck
bók	a servant, charioteer
bom	whichever, all
bóng	mugwort (*Artemisia vulgaris*)
bots	to bark
bou-you	a mayfly
bouh	big and fat
bóuh	to carry in the arms
bouk	to return
brák	white
brank	a pair
breng	peaceful
bront	beautiful
bróu	a gourd
brun	poor
buh	wife
buk	1. to think about
	2. to lie down
	3. a garment, robe
búm	bushy
bús	a netsuke; to wear hung from the sash
buy	fat, rich
chah	thorns
chah-chah	luxuriant, rich
cho	hay
dá	disabled
dak	great, stately
dán	a sandalwood tree
dang	a skirt, garment for lower part of body
dáng	a hall

dangs	top, on; to place on, add to
dant	an area of levelled ground for sacrifices
dánt	far-reaching
dap	to wade, cross a stream
dats	1. to swear, promise
	2. to move on, get as far as
dawk-ráwk	a peony
dáwks	sad
deh	this
deng	1. inner wall of a town, a walled town
	2. complete, perfect
díh	a younger brother
dít	1. old age
	2. to laugh scornfully
diwk	virtuous
djin	to arrive, reach
do	a kind of lance
dó	to throw
dók	alone
don	to hasten; quickly
dón	heavy (as dew)
dóng	1. together
	2. a boy, young man
dos	to plant
dóu	a stick with plumes attached
dóuk	poison
dóun	to tie together
dount	a shield
dous	to sell
douy	who?
dóuys	a metal cap on the butt of a shaft
doy	to hang down
dra	the area between a gateway and its screening wall
drah	ramie (*Boehmeria nivea*)
drang-chah	a starfruit tree
dre-dro	to walk haltingly
drék	to like
drók	muddy
drou	a nightdress
drou-mliw	to bind round
druks	to hold upright
druy	1. to dawdle

	2. an islet
druys	childish
du	fowl-hole in wall
dúk	really
dúnt	good
dúyh	variant pronunciation of *díh*, younger brother
dzá	to go to
dzang	a wall
dzans	to give a farewell feast
dzant	shallow; low-fenced; unmailed (horse)
dzén	in front
dzeng	affection
dzenk	quiet, pure
Dzin	Ch'in (State, later dynasty)
dzit	illness, pain
dzong	to follow
dzóunt	cherry salmon (*Oncorhyncus masou*)
dzóup	mixed
dzous	to get to
dzóyh	to sit
dzúh	at
dzún	to dwell at
dzúngs	to present
dzus	from
dzúyh	shepherd's-purse (*Capsella bursa-pastoris*)
en	how?
ént-ont	beautiful
ew	to agree a rendezvous
gá	how, why, what? *gá-nan*, how?
gáh	a door
gak-la	a rough bamboo mat
gámp	to rumble
gang	to act, practise
Gáy	the Yellow River; hence "river" generally
gáy	1. what?
	2. a lotus
gets	to foretell the future using milfoil stalks
gip	ten
gis	to regard
gláng	dodder
gláw	a peach
gloungs	a second son

gó	1. a marquis
	2. a target
gómp-lómp	a lotus flower
góng	a wild goose
gop	to join together
góps	to assemble; a meeting
got	to dig out
gou	an enemy
gouh	unlucky, inauspicious
goump	very
goun	a flock
goung	penury
góuts	turbulent, violent
grá	far; *pu grá A* "not far A": very likely, A
gráh	bottom, under, to descend
grák	to fall
gráks	1. dew
	2. a heron, egret
grang	cold
gráng	1. a road; to go
	2. a crossbeam
gránk	floating-hearts (*Nymphoides*)
gráp	familiar
grat	1. a hero
	2. a perch (for birds)
grát	an axle-cap with a linchpin
gráwk	joy, to rejoice in
grés-grós	happy and carefree
gróngs	a lane
grou	1. to pair, match
	2. to seek
grou-mrou	a triangular-bladed lance
gróuy	to cherish, yearn for
gru	a stipulated time
gu	1. his, her, its, their, your; *A gu B*, how B A is!
	2. black-mottled grey
guk	to the utmost; to get all the way to, go to the extreme
gum	a Chinese lute
gums	a sash or cord holding one's robe together
gup	1. together with
	2. to get to
guy	1. tall

	2. the area inside a door
gwá	a fox
gwang	foolish
gwáng	a reed-organ
gwát	1. alive
	2. to join
gweng	a precious stone
gwín	black
gwits	a shaking movement
gwráng	to plough crosswise
gwren	handsome
gwu	a fur garment
háh	a tiger
hangs	facing; south (i.e. facing the sun)
hánt	to scorch
hap	side of body
heng	a sound
hiw	crossboard of a chariot
hos	warm
hóuh	good
houk	to cherish
hóus	to love
hóuy	property, valuables
hóuy-lóuy	exhausted
houyh	rumble of thunder
hrák	fiery red, brilliant
hrouk	a store of vegetables
hung	to rise
huts	1. to collect
	2. to rest
huy	to dry in the sun
i	a syllable inserted for rhythm
ik	oh!
in	1. to rely on
	2. a mat
	3. a wall screening a gateway; *in tá*, the double gate in an outer town wall
it	one
íts	cloudy, windblown, dark skies
íwh-líwh	lovely
jah	1. precipitous, full of obstacles
	2. to find fault with

jin	a hazel
jos	to crinkle
jouh	wine
juk	side of the body
ka	a vehicle
ká	1. just for now
	2. father's sister
káh	1. a drum
	2. a merchant
kák	each
kám	sweet
kámp	to dare
kán	a rod, pole
káng	a ridge
kás	to look round
kát	the lablab bean (*Dolichos lablab*)
káw	high
káwh	white or undyed silk
káws	ointment
káy	to sing
ke	a branch
ké	a chicken
kék	to beat
kéns	to see
kéw	bright
kha	meek
khah	to stay
kháh	bitter
khak	red
khan	to tuck up one's skirt
khát	thirsty
kháyh	to be able to; *kháyh A*, A-able, worth A-ing
khét-khót	see *khót*
kho	to drive horses forward, gallop
khok	to bend; bent
khomp	a thump
khongs	to throw oneself on
khonk	to fear
khónk	greatly
khót, khét-khót	far apart
khóuh	to attain
khuh	a matrimony-vine (*Lycium chinense*)

khúk	to be able
khúks	skilful
khum	a coverlet
khúnk	to be willing
khup	dry, scorched
khúts	sad
khúyh	*khúyh A?*, how can A be? (it can't)
ki	fat, grease
kí	a hairpin
kih	fine-tasting
kit	luck, lucky
klháw	restless
klhoung	grieved, agitated
kloung	middle
kóh	a fish-trap
kók	1. a valley; *kók poum* "valley wind": the East wind
	2. alive
	3. the hub of a wheel
kómp	to touch, budge
kón	1. a cap
	2. to look
kóng	a prince; by extension, a palace
kóns	to pass through the centre of
kónt	a pipe
kós	to come across
kou	a pigeon
kóuh	bright
kouk	1. impoverished
	2. to address
kóuks	to announce
koump	a pillow
koun	a prince; *koun-tzuh*, "princely man"
koung	a palace, temple
kóunt	1. a cord
	2. a royal coat embroidered with dragons
kous	to save, rescue
kra	1. to stay
	2. a netsuke gem
krá	a home, family
kram-krá	rushes, sedge
krán	1. red-grass (*Themeda triandra*)
	2. an orchid

160

kráns	a stream in a ravine
kránt	nonchalant
krat-krat	sticking up vertically
kráw	1. to cross
	2. the edge of a town, a suburb
kráwh	crafty, perverse
kráy	1. to approve
	2. to hit the target
	3. a hairpin jewel
kráys	to yoke
krén	1. the space within or between something
	2. a lotus
krhan	to go past
krhat	warlike in appearance
krhats	to lift up one's clothes
krhup	to weep
krí	together; *krí róuh*, to grow old together (as a married couple), hence the one you grow old with, spouse
króh	if only
krók	a horn
krón	a barrier, barred gate
króns	the two tufts into which a child's hair was bound
kront	to roll; *kront-nuh* "rolled ears": mouse-ear chickweed
kros	a sandal, shoe
kroun	a fallow-deer
kroung	one's body, oneself
krum	gold
krump	silk woven in a coloured pattern, brocade
krun	a headcloth
krún	distress
kruy	hungry
krúy	cold
kuk	urgent
kum	now, today
kuts	*kuts A*, has already A-ed (and that's all)
kwá	a yellow horse with a black mouth
kwáng	1. light, brightness
	2. torrential water, fierce
kwát	to go together
kwáy	to transgress
kwayh	delapidated
kwét	a buckle

kwhán	broad
kwhang	a basket
kwhat	a watchtower over a gate
kwháy	beautiful
kwheng	slanted; *kwheng-kwhang* "slanted basket": a kind of basket used in harvesting
kwhenk	an unlined hemp garment
kwhu	a hill
kwóts	a Chinese juniper (*Juniperus chinensis*)
kwráng	a horn
kwrouh	the end of an axle
kwruh	nine
kwuh	1. a long time
	2. a gemstone, perhaps obsidian
kwúk	a nation
kwung	a bow (for shooting arrows)
kwuy	to go where one belongs, go home
la	1. I, we
	2. a falcon flag
lá	a dandelion
lah	1. with, and
	2. to give; *lah A*, for A
	3. open country
lak	pleased
laks	to shoot
lang	1. sunlight, sunny; *oum* and *lang*, Yin and Yang
	2. a poplar tree
	3. the forehead
	4. to raise; *lang-lang*, elated
lánk	smooth
lant	good
lap	a leaf
lat	a garment worn next to the skin
lats	slow-moving; dispersed
láts	big; *láts-pa*, a courtier, dignitary
law	a gemstone, perhaps jasper
lawk	to leap
lay	*A B lay*, A is B; *A lay*, as for A ...
láy	to flow
léks	false hair
leng	to fill; full

léng	the courtyard of a palace
lewk	a flute
léwk	a pheasant, pheasant feather
lha	to relax
lháh	earth
lhámp	young silvergrass
lhang	1. to injure, afflict
	2. heavily-flowing
lháng	reckless
lhap	the thimble used by an archer
lhát	1. to go to and fro
	2. the door of a room
lháy	other
lhet	to set in place
lhéwk	tapering
lhih	1. to swear
	2. an arrow
lhín	sky
lhot	to speak, to excuse
lhots	1. a kerchief
	2. to stop overnight
lhóts	easy, leisurely
lhouh	the head
lhouyh	water, a river
lhuh	to begin
Lhum	Orion's Belt
lhum	deep
lih	a pheasant
lin	to command
lins	traces (straps for pulling a carriage)
lit	fruit
liw	1. to long for; far away
	2. to flow
líw	long-drawn-out
lo	to overleap, to trespass
long, longs	to use
lonk	to jump
lot	1. a hole
	2. glad, satisfied
lou	to go along
lou-lou	pleased with oneself

louh	to entice
lóuh	a road, way
louk	to rear, nourish
lóung	red
louyh	the call of the female pheasant
lrák	a marsh
lray	1. a pond
	2. to gallop
lrhangs	long
lrit	pure
lrouk	to become prominent
lroung	insects
lu	to make a gift
lú	a tower, pagoda
luh	to cease
lúh	to come to, come to the time
luk	1. to eat
	2. a wing
	3. to shoot an arrow having a string attached
luks	different
lung	to mount
lúng	to oppress
lups	toil
lúy	a sprout
ma, mah	don't!
mah, mák, mang, mayh	hasn't, there isn't
mang	to disappear
mangs	to gaze at, admire
mank	1. a net
	2. to make a fool of someone
mans	to overspread; creepers
máw	an oxtail-pennon
máwks	to gather
mayh	see *mah*
meng	a name, fame
meyh	in full flow
mhúh	to regret
mhúk	black
mhúng	numerous
min	the people
mits	to fall asleep
móh	a Chinese acre

mók	1. a tree; *mók-kwrá* "tree-melon": a quince
	2. to wash one's hair
	3. an ornamental leather band round a carriage pole
móng	to cover
móng-nong	bushy, shaggy
mouh	male
mouk	an eye
moun	a design
móun	red millet
mouns	to ask, enquire about
mout	contraction of *mah tu*: *mout A*, don't A him
mouts	*mouts A*, hasn't yet A-ed
mrah	to dance
mráh	a horse
mrang	bright; *Mrang Séng* "the bright star": the Morning or Evening Star (the planet Venus)
mráng	1. the people
	2. snake's-head lily (*Fritillaria*)
mrángs	the eldest brother or sister
mrans	a scorpion
mráts	to proceed, march
mráy	hemp
mreng	to crow
mring	one's fate
mróng	a shaggy dog
mrós	to trade
mróu	cogon grass (*Imperata cylindrica*)
Mróuh	the Pleiades
mrú	a duststorm
mrúk	wheat
mrun	1. dusk
	2. marriage
mrunt-mrant	to exert oneself
mruy	the margin of a stream
mruyh	beautiful
mu	to plan, scheme
mú	1. a plum
	2. a go-between (to arrange marriages)
múh	mother
muk	pasture
múks	pain, distress
mún	a door, gate

mungs	a dream
múts	twilight
muyh	variant pronunciation of *mruyh*, beautiful
múyh	smooth-flowing
na, nak	like, as, if; *pu na* "not like": not as good as; *A na tu gáy*: how about A?, what is to be done about A?
na, nayh	you, your
na-ra	the madder plant
nah	angry
nak	that sort of
-nan	an adverb suffix: *A-nan*, A-ly
nang	heavy with dew
náns	difficulty, calamity
náyh	rich, fine
néng	why?
nga	a fish
ngá, ngan, ngáng	I, my, we, our
ngah	to speak
ngáh	five
ngaks	to set something out, serve a meal
ngam	majestic, grave
ngan	1. to speak
	2. at him/her/it, at that
	3. see *ngá*
ngáng	see *ngá*
ngans	a shore
ngas	face to face
ngás	to wake
ngáw	a pleasure-ground
ngáws	arrogant
ngay	right, proper; decorum; to make right, prepare something (e.g. for cooking)
ngáyh	me, us
ngets	to sow, plant
nghawk	to ridicule
ngins	to condole
ngo	a corner
ngok	jade
ngons	to long for
ngos	to encounter by chance
ngóu	to fly back and forth
ngrah	to withstand, prevent

ngrán	a colour
ngráns	a wild goose
ngrás	to meet
ngwa	to rejoice
ngwah	tall
ngwat	the moon, a month
ngwáts	outside
ngwu	a cow
nhán	to sigh
nhin	to prolong; to stay on in the same place
nhok	to bind, a bundle
nhouh	a hand
níms	to think about, remember
nin	a man, person
nit	the sun, a day
no	to wet
noung	a war chariot
nóup	the inner reins of the outside horses in a team of four
nouy	a tassel
nrah	a girl, woman
nu, nuh	A *nu* B, while A, B; although A, B
nú	1. to be able to
	2. to treat well
nuh	an ear
núm	south
nuyh	near
nuys	two; double-hearted
ók	a house
ons	to resent
ont	1. to elude
	2. beautiful, gentle
ós	to soak
ou	sad; grief
oum	shade, clouds; *oum* and *lang*, Yin and Yang
oump	to drink
óun	mild, gentle
oup	a town
ouy	to fear
oy-láy	compliant, submissive
pah	an axe
pang	1. a direction; *tóng pang*, *núm pang*, etc.: the East, the South, ...

	2. just now
	3. a raft
pant	1. a slope, bank
	2. to turn, reverse
pás	cloth
pát	to open something out, start out
pay	a river-bank
payh	that, they
pha	exhausted
pháng	heavy fall of snow, tears, etc.
pháns	1. a shore
	2. to dissolve
phih	to be separated
phong	a turnip
phóts	dense, luxuriant
phouk	to turn over, overthrow
phuks	a type of headdress
phuy	a heavy snowfall
phuyh	a radish
pit	must
pits	to give
pók	to foretell the future by making cracks in a shell or bone
pók-sók	undergrowth, low shrubby trees
pot	the hair of the head
pouh	pottery, a pot
poum	wind
póun	to run, elope
póus	to repay
pout	can't, won't
prák	1. a hundred
	2. the eldest brother, a chief; a woman's term for her husband; *prák tzih*, literally "eldest brother's elder sister": father's elder brother's daughter
prang	a weapon
prank	to hold, grasp
pránt	a plank
prhong	beautiful
pris	reins
prits	1. to close
	2. the shaft of a lance
	3. to bubble up from a spring
próng	a State

próu	to wrap
prung	ice
pruy	to grieve; sad
pu	not
puh	doesn't
púk	the back side, north
púks	the back
puy	to fly
puyh	isn't
ran	to fall, as tears
rang	1. fine; *rang-nin*, a good man, or lovely woman
	2. a carriage pole
	3. a dam
	4. a blossom, or a kind of precious stone
rángs	reckless, excessive
ráns	1. pleasant
	2. brilliant, burning
rats	to get one's clothes wet
ráw	toil
raws	to cure
ray	1. to fasten
	2. to depart from
re	a black horse
rhas	summer
rhíh	the body
rih	to tread
rin	sound of carriages rumbling
ríng	1. a plant species, probably cocklebur (*Xanthium strumarium*)
	2. to fall in drops
rit	a chestnut
ríw	may it be that ..., it will happen that ...
rók	1. a deer
	2. to moisten, smear
rong	a dragon
róns	to disturb; disorder, rebellion
rós	to engrave
rou	1. to catch
	2. to flow, drift apart
	3. a bay horse with black mane
rou-ray	an owl
rouh	deep and clear

róuh	old
rouk	1. six
	2. a plateau
róuy	1. a jar
	2. thunder
rú	to come
ruh	1. a plum
	2. a hamlet, homestead
	3. a carp
ruk	strength
rum	a forest
ruy	this; this alone
sah	to unburden
sak	in times past
sáks	white, white silk
sang	mutually
sáng	mulberry tree
saws	to laugh
sáyh	small (possibly a variant pronunciation of *sewh*?)
sdóuy	craggy; *sdóuy-ngóuy*, a rocky peak
sduk	clear, as water
sdus	a eunuch
sék	1. to split
	2. white
séng	a star
sent	rare, fine
sew	evening, night
sewh	small
sgoump	mulberry fruit
sgwan, sgwan-ngwan	a spring
shah	*A shah B*, that which A B's; a place where
shan	a mountain
sháng, shéng	green or blue (these are regarded by the Chinese as shades of the same basic colour)
sháng-ung	a fly
shank	to deviate
sheng	1. to be born, be alive
	2. a sister's child
shéng	see *sháng*
shong	a pair
shóum	the outside horses of a team
shóum-shay	uneven

shuh	to cause, make someone do something
shúh	to pluck
shúh-shúh	many-coloured
shús	vegetable, edible plant
sih	to die
sin	1. new
	2. firewood
sít	to consider something pure
sits	four; a team of four horses
siwk	swift
siwks	to embroider
síws	to wail
skong	a pine
slék	to give
sliw	dried-up
smáng	mourning, a burial
smángs	to lose, destroy
sngáks	to go upwards; *sngáks wúy* to go upstream, *sngáks you* to go downstream
snins	sincere, to trust
snouy	to walk slowly
so	to wait
sóngs	to accompany, escort someone
sont	to count, measure
sot	snow
sóu	to scratch
souk	1. to stay overnight
	2. early morning
sóum	three
souy	although
spits	snivel
sprit	a musical instrument having numerous strings stretched horizontally over a bridge, comparable to the harp
staks	1. may it be that ...
	2. numerous
stek	to fall in with
stit	a room, home
stiwk	third of four brothers or sisters
stos	to guard a border
su	1. silk
	2. to think
suk	to rest, repose

sum	the heart
sus	to brood
súy	1. west
	2. to roost; *súy-druy*, to relax, rest
súyh	washed clean
swat	a year of life
swin	truly
swit	to care for someone
ta	*ta A*, the A's
tá	the outer wall of a city; a capital city
tah	1. *A tah*, one who is A, one who A's, an A-er; as for A, ...
	2. an islet
	3. red pigment
táns	dawn
tat	to break
tats	bright
táts	a sash, belt
taw	to beckon
tawk	to pour wine
táy	many
teh	an empty filling-out word
téks	emperor, God
teng	1. to go on an expedition against
	2. the centre of a target
téws	to fish
thang	splendid
tháng	a drumbeat
théks	a hairpin
thi	fine cloth
thíh	tears; to weep
thín	an ornamental jade ear-stopper
tho	agreeable, compliant, lovely
thong	to fill
thoun	springtime
thóun	to groan
thout	to go out, exit
thóuy	motherwort
thu	jesting, jolly; *thu-thu*, a jokester
tín	1. the forehead
	2. to be overthrown
tint	black hair
tip	to grasp

tits	to get to
títs	chagrined
Tiw	name of the ruling dynasty (in Mandarin, Chou)
toks	a horse with a white left hind leg
tong	a bell
tóng	east
tou	1. a boat; *tou-tzuh*, a boatman
	2. an islet
touk	to bind
tóum	to indulge one's pleasures
toung	perpetual, all through
tóung	winter
trants	a ritual robe
traw	morning
tre	to know; someone you know well, an intimate friend
trent	truly
trent-tront	to toss and turn
trhangs	the case in which an archer keeps his bow
tris	to place
trits	to convey, transmit
trot	to gulp
trou	a carriage pole
trouk	bamboo
tsa	an earth-clad rock
tsa-kou	a fish-hawk
tsah	and; again
tsan	to move house
tsang	to request; please!
tsáns	a beauty-threesome
tsant	shallow
tsáyh	shining white
tseng	pure, clear
tseyh	1. this
	2. bright, lustrous
tsimp	to lie down to sleep
tsit	1. seven
	2. a lacquer-tree
tsiw	autumn
tso-tsang	to step in an agile, well-balanced manner, as in sport, ritual, or dance
tsongs	admittedly
tsos	to take a wife

tsou-lhay	a toad
tsóuh	grass, vegetation
tsúy	a wife
tsúy-tsúy	dense, luxuriant
tswats	a robe with figured top and embroidered skirt
tu	to go to
tu, tuh	him, her, it, them; *A tu B*, A's B, the B of A
tuh	1. to stop
	2. an islet
tuk	to ascend
túk	1. to get
	2. quality, character
tza	a verbal exclamation mark
tzáh	a cord
tzam	to moisten
tzang	1. to be about to
	2. to escort
tzáng	good, right
táng-táng	luxuriant (foliage)
tzay	alas!
tzáyh	left-hand
tzeng	a feather-pennon
tzewk	nobility, rank; a type of ritual vessel (Mandarin *chüeh*)
tzih	an elder sister
tzik	straight away
tzík	the joints in stems of plants such as bamboo
tzit	to go to
tzong	longways
tzóng	to bind together
tzoun	to follow a path
tzoungs	a multitude, all
tzu	this
tzú	a verbal exclamation mark
tzuh	a son, child, boy or girl; you; a gentleman, lady; *A-tzuh* "son of A": the person connected to A, e.g. *tou* "boat", *tou-tzuh* "boatman"
tzúk, tzúks	*A tzúk(s) B*, if A then B, because A therefore B; *A tzúk(s)*, ..., as for A, ...
tzúng	to hate
tzup	an oar
tzús	to travel in a carriage
tzúy	steep

tzúys	to ford
uh	a syllable inserted for rhythm
um	a sound, a message
un	great
ung	a breastplate
úts	to love
uy	this
uy, uy-buk	garment, particularly for upper part of body; *uy-dang* "jacket and skirt": clothes, dress (for either sex)
wa	to go to; to
wah	rain
wan	1. then
	2. to pull up
	3. a wall, a garden
wán-rán	the rough-potato plant (*Metaplexis*)
wang	king
wáng	leisure
wáng-wáng	brilliant
wank	to go towards
want	far
wants	to stay far from, to leave
wat	verbal inverted commas, introducing a direct quotation
way	to act as; to act for, help
ways	because
wé	to lead by the hand
wek	military service
wen	grieved
wéts	affectionate, to favour
wha	to grieve, alas!
whan	to forget
wháns	ample
whe	a horn or bone spike for opening knots
whéts	to jingle
whín	far away
wi	1. as for ...; is only; *wi zuh*, by this means
	2. a curtain
wít	a hole, pit
wóh	after; those who come after, descendants
wount	densely ornamented
wrah	a feather, a wing
wrangs	to wade
wrank	eternal

wrans	a beauty
wrén	a ring
wréng	a kind of precious stone
wrha	great
wrhá	flowers
wrhang	elder brother
wruk	a fishing net
wrun	to fall down
wu	to blame
wuh	1. to have, there is; very; *wuh na A*, "[I swear] by A!"
	2. a friend
	3. right-hand
	4. winding
wun	1. to say; *wun gáy*, "how, pray?"
	2. clouds
	3. an empty filling-out word
wung	male
wus	to repeat; further
wuts	to say
wuy	to go against, go away
wuyh	bright, blazing
yaks	a night
yang	a sheep
yang-yang	flowing abundantly
yong	1. the face
	2. a ceremonial dagger
you	1. still, yet; as, alike
	2. to swim, float, wander about
za	slow
zak	evening
zang	to go to and fro
zank	an elephant; hence, ivory; hence, carved, patterned
zhuh	1. to wait
	2. a riverbank
zih	a rhinoceros
zlok	a harness ring
zon	to turn round, return
zous	full dress
zouts	1. to progress, achieve
	2. a jade insignium carried at the girdle

zuh	to use; "to use it for" = in order to; *zuh A*, with A, by means of A; *zuh A waꞌ B*, to treat A as B, consider A to be B
zup	low, wet ground
zus	to continue

POWERFUL FOCUS

A 7-DAY PLAN TO DEVELOP MENTAL CLARITY
AND BUILD STRONG FOCUS

THIBAUT MEURISSE

CONTENTS

WHO IS THIS BOOK FOR?

Do you keep jumping from one task to the next? Do you struggle to stay focused long enough to achieve success? Is your mind all over the place?

If so, you need to develop Deep Focus.

More specifically, you'll find this book useful if you want to:

- Eliminate distractions and develop laser-sharp focus
- Stop jumping from one shiny object to the next
- Overcome information overload so that you can move forward with your goals
- Gain clarity about your goals so that you can focus on what matters
- And much more

So are you ready to develop unshakeable focus and get things done?

Your Free Step-By-Step Workbook

To help build unshakeable focus I've created a workbook as a companion guide to his book. Make sure you download it at the following URL:

https://whatispersonaldevelopment.org/powerful-focus

If you have any difficulties downloading the workbook contact me at:

thibaut.meurisse@gmail.com

and I will send it to you as soon as possible.

INTRODUCTION

The ability to focus is one of the most valuable assets you'll ever develop. When you use it to achieve your most exciting goals, you can reach levels of success you would never have imagined possible.

Often, the difference between an average person and a highly successful one is their level of focus. Successful people know what they want and place all their focus into the accomplishment of their goals. By doing so consistently over a long period of time, they turbocharge their productivity and achieve most of their goals.

What about you? Are you the master of your focus or the slave of distractions?

In *Deep Focus*, you'll learn how to move from distracted to laser-sharp focused in just seven days. Each day, you'll be given exercises to strengthen your focus. By the end of the seven days, you'll have developed a deeper understanding of what focus is, how focus works and you will be well on your way to becoming one of the most focused people you know.

In **Part I. Gaining Clarity**, we'll work on refining your vision. As you develop a clearer vision, you'll be better able to identify the key tasks to work on today, this week, and this month. The more clarity you gain, the easier it will be for you to focus. More specifically, we'll cover the following:

- **Day 1**—15 questions to identify what you want.
- **Day 2**—Gaining clarity regarding what you want.
- **Day 3**—Gaining clarity regarding what needs to be done.
- **Day 4**—Gaining clarity regarding how it needs to be done.

In **Part II. Eliminating Distractions and Obstacles**, you'll discover how to remove all the distractions around you and develop laser-sharp focus. You'll learn to simplify. As you do so, you'll feel more in control of your day. Here is what we'll cover:

- **Day 5**—Simplifying.
- **Day 6**—Reducing useless input.
- **Day 7**—Eliminating friction and energy waste.

Sounds good?

If so, let's get started, shall we?

PART I

GAINING CLARITY

I believe the number one reason we're so busy and restless is that we lack clarity. Therefore, one of the most important things to do to increase focus is to gain clarity regarding:

- What you want and why,
- What exactly you need to do to achieve your goals, and
- How to achieve your goals with maximum effectiveness.

In short, you need to know the why, the what, and the how.

That's what we're going to cover in this part. Without further ado, let's get started with Day 1.

DAY 1—15 QUESTIONS TO IDENTIFY WHAT YOU WANT

Know what you want. Clarity is power. And vague goals promote vague results.

— ROBIN SHARMA, WRITER.

Today, I would like you to spend time answering the 15 questions presented in this section. Don't worry if you can't find the right answers. There is no such thing as a perfect answer. Simply try your best to answer each question honestly.

The more time you spent answering them, the more clarity you'll gain. And, once again, the more clarity you have, the better it will be to focus and reach your goals.

The 15 questions are divided into three categories:

A. Eliciting your desire,

B. Finding your strengths and unique abilities, and

C. Uncovering your passion.

Let's get started.

A. Eliciting desire

1. What do you really, really want?

On the surface, this is a rather simple question. Yet, most of us haven't taken enough time to think about it. Using your action guide, write down anything that comes to mind. Make sure you include all your crazy goals and dreams. Don't limit yourself. Treat this as the brainstorming phase.

Now, look at your list. Identify your top two or three goals. Which of them do you really, really want above all the others?

2. If you were to wake up tomorrow, completely alone without any family member, friend, or colleague to influence your decisions, what would you do differently?

Your family members—especially your parents—or acquaintances may have led you to make the wrong decisions, such as choosing the wrong career or dating the wrong person. Imagine you could do anything you wanted without anyone judging you. What would you do differently?

3. If you were to be totally honest with yourself, what would you start doing now and what would you stop doing?

Spend a few minutes to focus on what you want, deep down. Is what you're currently doing today what you really want to do? If you keep doing what you're doing today, this week or this month, will you be where you want to be five or ten years down the line? In short, are you focusing on the right things?

4. If you were guaranteed to succeed in everything you do, where would you want to be in three years?

Let go of any mental limitations. What's the best possible place you could be mentally, physically, spiritually, and financially in three years? Do you want more freedom? Do you want to find the right partner? Do you want to pursue a career you love? Write down everything you want.

5. If you could spend your day exactly the way you wanted to, what would you be doing from morning to night? What would your ideal day consist of?

Close your eyes and imagine yourself during your ideal day. What does it look like? What time do you wake? What do you eat for breakfast? What activities do you engage in? Who do you spend time with? In which country or city are you living and in what kind of house?

The more clarity you have, the better.

Remember, people who define their life goals are more likely to achieve them than those who don't. This is because they know what they need to focus on every day. Do you?

To clarify your vision further, don't hesitate to run through this exercise over and over in the coming weeks or months.

6. If you could focus only on doing one thing for the rest of your life, what would it be?

Although you might struggle with this question, try to answer it as best you can. What one thing could you possibly commit to doing for the rest of your life? Pick just one thing, and make sure it's the most important thing to you.

7. If you understood and truly believed you could achieve absolutely anything you want by sticking to it for long enough, what would you pursue for the next three to five years?

What is the one goal you want to achieve the most right now? What really excites you? Could you do whatever it takes for as long as necessary until you achieve it?

By now, you should have a better idea of what you want. Feel free to review these questions as often as you need to. Clarity needs to be refined over time. Don't expect to find the right answer the first time and don't forget, it's possible to change it whenever necessary.

B. Finding your strengths and unique abilities

Identifying your strengths and working from them is one of the most important things you can do to ensure you place your focus where it should be. If you spend your days doing the things you are poor or mediocre at, you'll never achieve extraordinary results, and you will probably feel miserable as a result. Therefore, identify your strengths and use them as often as possible.

Also, remember that, when sustained over a long period of time, your focus will lead to exponential results. You will get far better results when you invest your time and effort doing what you excel at.

Think about it this way:

Would you rather magnify your strengths or your weaknesses?

What would be the long-term consequences of doing one versus the other?

The following questions will help you discover your biggest strengths and your unique abilities:

8. When you are the happiest at work, what are you doing?

You may love your job or hate it, but there will probably be times when you feel happy and engaged in the tasks you perform. Over the coming week, start noticing these moments. What are you doing specifically? And what does this say about your strengths and passions?

9. What do you find so easy that you genuinely wonder why others struggle to do the same thing?

Perhaps your communication skills are excellent. Perhaps you're a great listener. Perhaps you can explain complex topics in simple terms. However, because these skills come so easily to you, you may not see them as important attributes.

From experience, I can tell you, if every day feels like a struggle, you're probably not acting from your strengths. If this is the case with you, spend extra time identifying your strengths. Then, act on them and things will become easier.

10. What do people around you say you're great at?

What do other people compliment you on? What do they say you're good at? It's often easier for people who know you to identify your strengths than it is for you to do it yourself. This is because you have many blind spots and need an external point of view. One thing you can do is send a message to your family, friends, and colleagues and ask them to share what they think your biggest strengths are. If necessary, you could use the template below:

Hi_____,

How are you?

I'm trying to identify my strengths so I can use them to design a more fulfilling career and life. I need your perspective on what you consider I am really good at.

I'd really appreciate if you could provide me with honest feedback and give me a list of the strengths you think I have.

Please don't be afraid to tell me anything that comes to mind.

Thanks so much for your support.

Warm regards,

For instance, several people have told me that I have a gift for making difficult concepts easy to understand. I could have chosen not to make any further effort to improve my craft. However, this is not what I chose to do. On the contrary, I decided to focus on this "gift" and hone my skills until I become the best I can be.

Below are two comments I received from my readers in this regard:

"You have a great gift for synthesizing information into pure crystal clarity."

"You have the gift of presenting this subject in the simplest of terms, which I am finding quite profound."

What about you? What are your special gifts?

C. Uncovering your passion

Do you know what you're passionate about? If not, this section will help you identify your passions. Make sure you take enough time to answer the following questions fully.

11. What did you enjoy doing when you were a kid?

Often, what we did when we were kids reveals certain aspects of our personality. As time passes, we tend to become distracted by life (school, sport, or video games). As a kid, I used to read a lot. Sometimes, I read throughout the day. When I was eight, I used to write short stories. Ironically, it took me over twenty years to return to writing, which is something I would never have predicted.

It's your turn now. What did you enjoy doing when you were a kid?

12. Who do you envy and why?

Being envious of other people generally means they have something you want. I used to be jealous of successful personal development bloggers. I wanted to do the same thing they were doing. This led me to start a personal development blog and later to write books like this one.

So, who do you envy and what are these people doing? What do they have that you want, and what does this say about your passions?

13. If you had all the time and money in the world, what would you do?

This question removes issues most people have, like lack of time and money. It also gives you an opportunity to think about what you want to do more creatively and without boundaries. Most people believe that if they had tons of money, they would retire and live happily ever after. However, in truth, they would most likely grow bored and would need to find activities that bring them fulfillment, lest they end up unhappy with their so-called perfect life.

What about you? What would you do in such a situation?

14. If you had complete confidence and were already your absolute best self, what would you be doing with your life?

This question helps remove any sense of limiting fear, and it can also help you find clarity on what you really want to do. Remember, your best self is already within you. As you start believing in yourself and envisioning who you want to be, you'll begin to act differently. So, what does the confident you look like and what is he or she doing?

15. How do you want to express yourself to the world?

Do you want to entertain, educate, inspire, heal, teach or create? What emotions do you want people to feel as a result of the work you're doing? This question helps clarify your means of expression and how you want to serve the world.

In the end, I believe we are all here to express ourselves fully. Discovering our passion means expressing ourselves in an authentic way and sharing our gifts with the world.

What is your gift and how do you want to share it?

* * *

Action step

Using your action guide, answer the questions above. If you can't answer all of them today, that's fine. Just do your best. You can revisit them later and refine your answers as necessary.

DAY 2—GAINING CLARITY REGARDING WHAT YOU WANT

Lack of clarity is the primary reason for failure in business and personal life.

— BRIAN TRACY, AUTHOR.

Hopefully, by now, you should have a little more clarity regarding your long-term goals. If not, don't worry. Creating a vision is an on-going process that may require many repetitions.

Today, let's look at your current goals and assess how well they fit into the bigger picture. To do so, using your action guide, write down your career goals, financial goals, relationship goals, health goals, and personal goals.

Now, are these goals what you really, really want? Or are they goals imposed on you by your external environment (peer pressure, expectations from your parents, et cetera)?

Many people unknowingly pursue goals that aren't theirs, and they pursue them for the wrong reasons.

Love-based vs. fear-based goals

A simple model you can use to identify whether you're doing the right thing is the love-based vs. fear-based model. At any time, we're either acting out of love or out of fear.

When we act out of love, our focus is on giving. We're trying to add something to the world by giving our time, money, or attention, or by sharing our knowledge and attempting to help others.

On the other hand, when we act out of fear, our focus is on *getting*. We're trying to take something from the world. We want to take other people's money, use their work and pick their brains without giving anything in return. Or we seek to acquire fame or *get* that person we fancy.

At a deeper level, love-based behaviors come from a place of abundance. When we act out of love, we communicate to the world that we have enough, we are enough and we are happy to contribute to the world around us. Conversely, fear-based behaviors come from a place of scarcity. When we act out of fear, we tell the world (and ourselves) that we aren't enough and we don't have enough, therefore we must take as much from the world around us as we can before it's too late. When we do so, we are being controlled by ego.

Because fear-based goals are an attempt to *get* fulfillment and validation from the external world, they make for poor goals. On the other hand, love-based goals come from within and, as such, they are much more powerful. They enable us to express ourselves and share with the world who we truly are and what we believe in.

For example, acting out of love could be working on something you enjoy with the intent of helping other people. Acting out of fear could be pursuing a goal in order to impress other people. See the difference? It's hugely important.

Now, it's never one or the other. In truth, we tend to alternate between fear-based and loved-based behaviors throughout our day. Accordingly, don't beat yourself up if you catch yourself acting out of fear. Notice it and try to refocus on love-based behavior.

So, are your current goals really yours? Are they allowing you to express yourself fully, or are they an attempt to win other people's approval?

* * *

Action step

Using your action guide, write down what you really want to achieve. Make sure it is aligned with your personality and values, and that it genuinely excites you. Imagine you didn't have to please anybody and didn't need to become famous or look cool. In this case, what goals would you go after?

Imagine you could never share your accomplishments with anybody else, what goals would make you proud of yourself regardless?

DAY 3—GAINING CLARITY REGARDING WHAT NEEDS TO BE DONE

It's a lack of clarity that creates chaos and frustration. Those emotions are poison to any living goal.

— STEVE MARABOLI, WRITER.

Put simply, achieving a goal is about closing the gap between where you are and where you want to be. The key question then is, how do you do close the gap as quickly and effectively as possible? There's no point in wasting your time by focusing on ineffective tasks or adopting poor strategies. You want each of your actions to be impactful and move the needle forward, don't you?

Assess where you are right now

A great question I like to ask myself is:

"If I keep doing what I'm doing today, this week, or this month, am I likely to achieve my goals?

I know that if the answer is "no" for too many days, I need to do something to change the situation. I need to refine my strategy and ensure that I'm working on the right things each day. Otherwise, I will never reach my final destination.

While this may seem common sense (and it is), many people fail to work on the key tasks that will help them achieve their goals. The main reason is that these tasks are usually the most challenging ones. As a result, they'd rather do anything else but tackle them.

Below are some key questions to ask yourself:

- Am I really working on the challenging tasks I know I should be working on?
- If so, am I doing it consistently?
- Do I actually know what I need to do to reach my goals?

If your answer to these questions is no, let's work on it today.

Action step

Select a major goal you want to focus on. Now, ask yourself: If I keep doing what I've been doing today or this week, will I achieve this goal? If not, what do I need to change? Write down your answer using your action guide.

Then, come up with a specific strategy to achieve that goal. To do so, consider the following:

- Who has achieved a similar goal already?
- Is there a book or course I could access to help me achieve my goal?
- What few things should I focus on to reach my goal?

Do your best to answer the above questions. You can keep revising your strategy over time. Remember, you cannot achieve a goal if you don't know the steps you need to follow to reach it.

To learn how to be more strategic with your goals in greater depth, refer to the next book in this series, **Book 4**, *Strategic Mindset*.

DAY 4—GAINING CLARITY REGARDING HOW IT NEEDS TO BE DONE

Clarity affords focus.

— Thomas Leonard, life coach.

Many people fail to achieve their goals, not because they don't work hard enough, but because their strategy is inaccurate, unclear or plain wrong. To increase the odds of reaching any goal in life, you must develop what I call "an accurate model of reality". In other words, you must strive to make correct assumptions that will help you take the right actions and obtain the desired results. If your assumptions are inaccurate, you either won't be able to achieve tangible results or will have to work significantly harder to do so.

As a writer, I see many of my peers wasting time on ineffective tasks as a result of holding the wrong assumptions. For instance, one assumption often relayed by so-called marketing gurus is the idea that authors should be everywhere. If you're continuously promoting your books, you'll end up selling a lot of them, right?

Therefore, you should seize every opportunity to market your books by:

- Advertising your books on Amazon, Facebook, or Instagram,
- Giving podcast interviews,
- Having a social media presence on YouTube, Facebook, LinkedIn, Pinterest, Instagram, TikTok, and more,
- Organizing seminars or webinars,
- Organizing book launch parties,
- Partnering with other authors, and so on.

While there is nothing wrong with any of the activities above, it doesn't mean that you, as an author, should be doing all of them.

Considering how competitive the online space is, as an aspiring writer with few resources and limited time, there is no way you can do all the things above.

But the real lesson is that you shouldn't even try to do them all.

Strategically speaking it doesn't make sense. In truth, you should clearly define your strategy and goals as a writer (or an artist, or a musician). Then, you should decide the most effective moves for you based on your situation, the resources available (how much time and/or money you have), and your personal preferences (whether you're an introvert or extrovert).

1. The 80/20 Principle

When it comes to productivity, one key thing to understand is The 80/20 Principle, which states that twenty percent of your actions will generate eighty percent of your results. Of course, it's not an exact science, but it works for almost anything in varying degrees. Perhaps just one percent of your output creates fifty percent of your results. Or perhaps, thirty percent of your actions account for ninety percent of your outcome. The real key is to identify your high-impact tasks.

For instance, despite what book marketers recommend, I only focus on a few activities. I'm barely active on social media, and I haven't posted anything on Facebook, LinkedIn, or Twitter for months. I sometimes give interviews, but only rarely. And I don't try to sell my books at events.

Here's what has been working for me:

- Writing books consistently,
- Advertising them mostly using Amazon ads, and
- Building an email list of readers.

That's it.

Now, I'm not saying this is what every author should do. I'm just saying that this is what works for me, and for any author, there are probably a few activities that will work very well.

If they try to do everything, their actions will have little power and they won't be able to generate enough traction to gain the visibility and momentum needed to sell many books.

Here is one of my favorite quotes by the marketer, Seth Godin, "*A woodpecker can tap twenty times on a thousand trees and get nowhere but stay busy. Or he can tap twenty thousand times on one tree and get dinner.*"

If you're feeling overwhelmed, jumping from one activity to the next, but never achieving tangible results, it's probably because you've been ignoring The 80/20 Principle.

2. Strategy vs. tactic

Another major trap is to mistake tactics for strategies. These are *not* the same thing and understanding the difference between the two is critical.

A strategy is a carefully crafted set of tactics that, when combined, lead to the achievement of a specific goal. A good strategy implies that each tactic must work synergistically in a way that dramatically increases the odds of success.

On the other hand, a tactic is a specific action that is part of an overall strategy. That is, a tactic shouldn't be taken independently. Its effectiveness comes from being combined intelligently with other tactics that are part of the same overall strategy.

The point is a tactic must always be considered as part of a strategy. Many people use one tactic after the next without having identified a clear strategy first. This is a big mistake.

For instance, new authors hearing a book marketer recommending Instagram, may open their account right away. Or they may create Facebooks ads right after seeing an author having tremendous success with them. And they will keep trying new tactics over and over. Unfortunately, it is highly unlikely they'll succeed by using this scattergun method. Most people act this way because they believe there is a magic pill, and to be successful, all they need to do is find it.

Instead, an author with a sound strategy will be much more deliberate. For instance, they may decide to create an ongoing series and put most of their marketing effort into promoting the first book in the series. Then, they may choose to focus on running Facebook ads, optimizing their ads relentlessly until they're profitable.

Or imagine you want to run your own restaurant. You must have a solid strategy so you can choose effective tactics aligned with that strategy. Just mixing tactics you've heard from other restaurant owners won't work.

Instead, you would ask yourself, what type of restaurant will you open? A fast food or a high-end restaurant? How will you differentiate yourself from your competitors? Will you offer an outstanding service? Stunning ambiance? A large variety of dishes? And how will you attract customers?

Of course, you may need to experiment before you find what works best for your particular business. But make sure that, once you do, you also identify the key tactics that form part of this strategy. Then, at all costs, avoid being distracted by anything not part of the overall strategy.

3. Have one business model

Another common issue is trying to implement multiple business models at once. For example, many non-fiction writers lack clarity regarding what they want their books to do for their business. For example:

- Do they want to make money directly from their books?
- Do they want to use their books as a tool to promote their training courses or coaching services?
- Do they want to use their books to build their credibility?
- Do they want to land paid speaking gigs?

If, to begin with, they don't choose one strategy, they are likely to scatter their effort and struggle to have any kind of success.

Personally, I chose to make money with my books relying mostly on Amazon. This suggests that I must write books consistently and advertise them effectively via Amazon ads. If I had chosen to use my books to sell courses or coaching services, I would have acted differently. I would have spent a lot of time creating an effective sales funnel and would have likely written fewer books.

Now, does this mean you cannot do several of the above? No, of course not, but I would recommend that you focus on one specific business model and stick to it. Once you achieve the desired results, you might be able to implement one more. This is especially true if you have the money to outsource certain tasks or build a team. But start with one model.

Obviously, I'm giving you these examples because, as a writer, it's what I know best, but the same logic applies for any other business idea or goal you want to pursue.

What about you? Are you trying to pursue several business models or strategies at once? If so, how could you revise your strategy to increase its effectiveness?

4. Get rid of feel-good activities

Do you spend most of your time and effort on your most impactful tasks or do you allow yourself to get distracted by ineffective tasks?

Many people work hard to avoid hard work. What's the difference you may ask?

Working hard means keeping yourself busy, trying to complete as many tasks as possible. On the other hand, doing hard work means focusing most of your time and effort on the difficult tasks that move the needle. People who can perform hard work consistently will achieve great results. People who merely work hard may not.

To develop deep focus and achieve most of your goals, you must separate the two. You must be especially wary of doing what I call "feel-good activities".

Feel-good activities are activities that give you the illusion you're making progress (when you aren't). We often engage in such activities as a way to avoid facing the hard work. It's a sort of hidden procrastination.

Some examples of feel-good activities could be:

- Spending hours tweaking your company logo,
- Working on ineffective tasks that have little to no impact, and
- Working on projects that don't fit into your overall strategy.

Feel-good activities give you the impression of moving forward. As such, they are a major trap. But what you want isn't to feel good by completing minor tasks—it is to feel great by completing major tasks.

Below are some examples of what I mean by hard work:

- Cold-calling clients to land new contracts that will increase your revenue.
- Writing books that will attract new readers and increase your sales.
- Attracting coaching clients that will increase your bottom line.
- Working on improving your key products or services to deliver more value to your customers.
- Improving your sales page or sales pitch to boost conversion.

I believe that deep down, you'll almost always know what you *should* be doing. You're just too afraid of doing it so you distract yourself in all sorts of ways. But I would challenge you to stop working hard and start doing hard work instead. Yes, hard work *is* more demanding. It will use more of your mental energy, and it might be scary at times. However, as you practice doing hard work consistently, you'll see your results skyrocket.

5. Reduce your learning curve

Time is one of our scarcest resources. As such, you don't have time to reinvent the wheel. Whatever you want to accomplish, you must find ways to do it better and faster—more effectively. The better your blueprint is, the more you can direct your focus toward the most efficient activities and work on them consistently.

Here are the two things you need to focus on to reduce the learning curve:

1. Find the right information relevant to what you're trying to do or learn, and
2. Get help from people who've already achieved your goals (or similar ones).

In truth, whatever you're trying to achieve, there are people out there who've done it before. Learn from them.

1) Find the right information

To achieve the desired results, you must act on the right information, but in a world flooded with information, this is easier said than done. The first step to finding the correct information is to define your learning goals as clearly as possible. This entails knowing:

- **What exactly you're trying to learn.** To stay focused, keep in mind what you're trying to do. Make sure the tasks you're working on are important. Whenever you need to do research, clearly define the scope of your research to avoid overlearning and distractions.
- **Why exactly you need to learn it.** Before you tackle a task, ask yourself why you're doing it. How does it fit the big picture? Is it the best way to move closer to your goals?
- **What you want the final result to look like.** Define in

detail what you want the final result to look like. This will ensure you approach your tasks or project the right way.

2) Get help from people who've already achieved your goals

There are people out there who have already achieved the same goals you're targeting. There is no need to try to work it all out on your own.

You can interview these people, read their books or consume their content. As you do so, try to identify the blueprint you need to follow to reach your goal.

If you know someone who has already achieved your goals, I encourage you to "interview" him or her. Ask the following questions:

- What was your learning strategy?
- What was your single most effective activity?
- What did you with struggle the most and how did you overcome it?
- If you needed to learn that skill all over again, what would you do differently today?
- If you were in my shoes, how would you go about learning it?
- Is there anything else I should know?

The answers to these questions should help you create a significantly more effective plan.

Remember, to develop deep focus, you must know what to focus on. Asking people who have been and there done that is an effective way to do so.

PART II

ELIMINATE DISTRACTIONS AND OBSTACLES

How many hours do you work every week? While the typical workweek is forty hours, nobody actually works that amount of time. Most employees work fifteen to twenty hours at best.

In 2017, a study conducted by Voucher Cloud—a major UK money-saving brand—revealed that the average UK office worker is productive for only two hours and fifty-three minutes each day (or about one third of the time spent at the office). And this is likely to be the same for office workers all over the world.

The point is, these days most office workers are continuously distracted and have very little time each day to focus. Usually, they waste a lot of time by:

- Checking their emails or going on social media,
- Working on unimportant tasks that have little to no impact on their productivity, and
- Being continuously interrupted during their day.

To develop deep focus, you must eliminate distractions and remove any obstacle that prevents you from developing a deep state of concentration. As you learn to develop deep focus, you'll significantly increase your productivity, and often beyond anything you can imagine.

The first thing to boost focus is to simply stop doing as many unproductive activities as possible. Let's see how you can do this.

DAY 5—SIMPLIFYING

The ability to simplify means to eliminate the unnecessary so that the necessary may speak.

— HANS HOFMANN, PAINTER.

1. Practice ruthless elimination

To simplify your day, you must practice what I call "ruthless elimination". You need to eliminate the things that don't truly matter so that only the key tasks remain.

A. Practice zero-based thinking

An effective way to practice "ruthless elimination" is to use zero-based thinking, which is a technique that enables you to identify unproductive activities and remove them from your schedule. To use this technique, simply answer the questions below:

Knowing what I know now, would I choose to start that activity today?

For example:

- Knowing what I know now, would I still start this project?
- Knowing what I know now, would I still join that group?
- Knowing what I know now, would I still create that product or service?

You must understand that everyone makes choices every day. Whatever activity, goal, or project you're working on, you're recommitting to it each day whether you're aware of it or not. Now, there's no rule saying that you can't eliminate certain activities and replace them with more effective or enjoyable ones, but it may not always seem that way if you've been involved in them for a long time.

For instance, perhaps, you run a book club, sit on a committee, or volunteer at your local church. These may be great and even charitable endeavors, but they may not be what you want to do anymore. Sometimes, the hardest thing to do is to let go of something good, to let yourself pursue something great. Do you still want to continue with the activity you've been pursuing for years? Is it the most important use of your time right now or could there a better and more fulfilling way for you to use your precious time?

Only you can answer these questions. Only you can choose what you really want to focus on, moving forward. The key is to be totally honest with yourself.

A cognitive bias called the "sunk cost fallacy" explains why we act this way. Having already spent so much time or effort on something, we find it hard to let go and move on. But such attachment to the past often prevents us from designing a better future. It traps our energy into activities that no longer make us happy or productive.

One of my friends, who is also a writer, struggles with this issue. While he's very creative and has a lot of ideas for future books, he finds himself stuck in the past, using tons of energy revising older books, hoping to increase his sales. As a result, he has begun to feel overwhelmed and unmotivated. This is because he fails to focus his creative energy on future projects.

I'm the opposite. I seldom go back and try to turn an unsuccessful book around. Instead, I accept that some books will not sell no matter how much time and effort I put into them. I let go and use my energy to create more books. Now, I'm not saying this is always the best thing to do. There may be a time when revisiting and improving past projects might be worth it, but it often isn't the case.

The same thing can be said of any activity or project. Understand that when you give your time and energy to an activity, you're implicitly recommitting to it every day. If it's not what you want to do, then it might be time to eliminate it, to free up energy, and move on.

B. Blank slate technique

Another technique you can use is the "blank slate technique". Usually, when we try to simplify our schedule, we look at all our activities, trying to identify which ones to eliminate. Now, the blank slate technique entails doing the opposite—it entails identifying the tasks you should add to your schedule.

To apply this technique, recreate your schedule from scratch. Imagine it is blank and ask yourself what you would add to it. Weigh each activity carefully and only add the vital ones. Consider it your minimum viable schedule.

To give you an analogy, my computer recently broke down and I had to buy a new one. Now, I could have transferred all the files to my new computer, but I choose not to. Instead, I decided only to add the files I'm actually using. In short, I chose to start from a blank slate and used it as an opportunity to reorganize my files.

What about you? If you had total permission to eliminate any activities you don't want to dedicate time to anymore and could implement the most minimalist schedule possible, what would it look like?

C. Learning to say no

Another way to eliminate activities and free time is "simply" by learning to say no more often. Time is one of your most precious assets and nobody is entitled to it but you. Interestingly, while time is more valuable than money, people act as though the opposite applies. They give their time freely and let others interrupt them, but they would never give their money away to whoever asked for it, would they?

Learning to say no is a sign of self-respect. It means you respect yourself enough to focus on things that truly matter to you while saying no to less important activities.

If you struggle to say no, consider the following:

1. **Your life is made up of time.** Whenever someone "borrows" your time, they're stealing a part of your life. Remember that nobody has the right to steal your time without your consent. Of course, it doesn't mean you can, or should, say no to everything and never help others, but it does mean that you should be more selective and that you must learn to value your time more than anything else.

2. **Your time must be used in a meaningful way.** When you say yes to everything, you're disrespecting yourself and neglecting your goals and values. As a result, you end up living a life far below your potential, and you fail to give your gifts to the world and express yourself the way you were supposed to. To make it easier to decline requests, refine your vision, and identify your

core values. Doing so will help you weigh each request for your time carefully and assess whether you should accept or decline them.

Below are some techniques to help you say no:

Make "no" your default answer. For most people, the default answer is "yes". They only say no when they muster enough courage to do so. I encourage you to do the opposite and say "no" by default. Then, assess each request carefully. If the request is aligned with your goals or values, or if it excites you, say yes. If not, consider declining the request.

Know what you value and broadcast it to the world. When you clearly know what's important to you, saying no will become easier. For instance, in a conversation, don't be afraid to mention that you promised to spend time with your kids or that you need to work on an important project. It's hard for people to argue against the things you value the most. How could they say that spending time with your kids isn't important or that your important project can wait? Occasionally, they may have to wait, but most often they won't. Also, the more you live by your values, the more people will respect you—and your time.

Practice saying no unapologetically. Many of us feel bad for rejecting someone's invitation and can't help justifying ourselves. I challenge you to say no *without* trying to justify yourself. For instance, you could say something like, "Thank you for the invitation but I'll pass this time."

Practice role-playing. Whenever you're thinking of declining a future request, role-play the whole situation either on your own, or (if you can) with someone else. To do so, visualize the actual situation and imagine what the person asking you for something would say. See them asking you to join a party, take on a project or help them out with something. Then, say out loud what you will tell them. You can also write your answer down.

When declining an invitation, you can use one or more of the following tactics:

- **Acknowledge their invitation.** For instance, you could say, "Sounds like fun but I'm afraid I have to pass this time".
- **Give a specific reason.** While you don't necessarily have to justify yourself, on some occasions, such as at work, it might be effective to mention a specific reason. For instance, you could say, "I can't work on it now because I have an important deadline and I'm already struggling for time."
- **Give a reason they can't argue with.** As we've seen before, it's hard for people to challenge your values or mission. For example, you could say, "Sounds like a good idea, but I promised my kids I'd spend time with them tonight. I'll have to pass this time but have fun."
- **Offer an alternative.** If you genuinely want to spend time with the person making the request, you can offer an alternative that will work better for you. For example, you could say, "I can't join the party tonight, but what about grabbing a coffee later this week?"

Be hard to reach. Many people willingly accept being interrupted many times during the day. They seem to be available to everyone who contacts them. By doing so, they're effectively telling others their time doesn't matter, that they're not up to big things. And because they have little respect for their own time, people will see them as having little respect for themselves. Therefore, instead of reacting to people around you, set your own rules and reach out to others when you choose to. For instance, I never answer my phone unless I know the number. And even so, I may not answer if it's during my peak hours in the morning. In fact, the other day, I received a call from a friend but didn't answer because I was writing. Some might say I was being rude, but when I returned my friend's call later, he understood my reason.

The point is, saying no is your right. In fact, the most successful people on this planet say no to almost everything. If you can't say no right now, how will you say no when you become more successful?

2. Minimize distraction

Distractions destroy your focus, making you far less competent than you really are. To develop laser-sharp focus you must eliminate or at least minimize all your distractions. We can differentiate two types of distractions as follows:

- Internal distractions, and
- External distractions.

Let's look at each one briefly.

A. Internal distractions

How often are you distracted and procrastinate due to a thought? Probably more often than you realize. Perhaps, it is the thought that you should reply to an email you forgot to answer. Perhaps it is the thought that you have time and can do that task later. Or perhaps it is the thought that you want to have a coffee or go for a walk.

When you work on complex tasks, your mental chatter is often your biggest enemy. You can always find excuses to do everything but the tasks that truly matter. So, how do you make your mental chatter work for you, not against you? One effective way to do so is to implement a daily morning routine. The point of such routines is to lower your level of stimulation and train your mind to work on challenging tasks. To do so you should:

Avoid distractions wherever possible. Don't start your day by checking your phone, going on the internet, or watching videos. These are highly stimulating activities. Once you engage in them, you'll have a tough time focusing on your most important tasks. Your mind will keep telling you that you can work on the difficult tasks later, steering you toward more exciting (and easier) tasks.

Engage in relaxing activities. Put yourself in a calmer and more focused state of mind. There are many ways to do this, but they include:

- Practicing deep, slow breathing,
- Meditating,
- Listening to relaxing music,
- Practicing mindfulness, and
- Stretching.

Then, begin working on your most important task.

Eliminate highly distracting tasks. To enhance your focus, identify the tasks that have the most "distracting power" for you. For me, it's YouTube.

While most people seek to add more things to their day, I would suggest that the opposite is more beneficial. I contend that deep focus (and high-level productivity) only occurs when there is nothing more to add. Once you've eliminated most distractions and put yourself in a focused state, you'll become much more productive.

B. External distractions

While internal distractions are self-created, external distractions are the result of your external environment. The more you optimize your external environment to avoid interruptions, the better your focus will be. External distractions are interruptions include:

- Phone and social media notifications,
- Phone calls,
- Colleagues dropping by your office for a chat,
- General noise, or
- A disorganized workspace.

It is impossible to focus if you're continuously being interrupted. To reduce external distractions, eliminate interruptions as much as possible. For example, you can block time to work on your key task while asking others not to disturb you. You can arrive at the office early, before your colleagues. Or, if you work from home, you can work while everyone else in your family is asleep.

In addition, make sure you remove any notifications on your phone. You can also ask your colleagues not to disturb during certain hours of the day or you can wear headphones to signal you're busy. Whatever works for you is fine but strive to get rid of external distractions at all costs. This is how you'll develop deep focus.

Action step

Complete the following exercises in your action guide:

1. Practice ruthless elimination

A. Practice zero-based thinking

- Make a list of all the activities you're engaging in in a typical week.
- Then, ask yourself the following question: Knowing what I know now, would I still engage in this activity? You can also do the same for projects you're working on, products or services you're offering, and so on.

B. Implement the blank slate technique

Imagine you could create your schedule from scratch while having the total freedom to eliminate any activity you wish. Write down in your action guide what your new minimalist schedule would look like.

C. Learning to say no

Using your action guide, write down what you could say "no" to next time and how exactly you'll decline the request.

2. Minimize distraction

A. Internal distractions

In your action guide, write down two or three specific things you will do to reduce internal distractions.

B. External distractions

In your action guide, write down two or three specific things you will do to reduce external distractions.

DAY 6—REDUCING USELESS INPUT

The art of being wise is the art of knowing what to overlook.

— WILLIAM JAMES, PHILOSOPHER.

Do you often feel overwhelmed, not knowing where to start? Do you feel stuck, unable to move forward with your tasks or projects?

If so, it's probably because you're absorbing too much unnecessary information. Sure, learning is important, but when you're spending too much time learning, you'll end up feeling overwhelmed and confused.

By learning more and digging ever deeper, you'll:

- Get lost in detail, losing sight of the big picture (missing the forest for the trees). Instead of having a decent grasp of the overall picture, you'll find yourself reading highly technical reports full of stats and anecdotes that you probably don't need to know. Ironically, as you keep doing so, you'll often end up absorbing less and less of the essence of what you're trying to learn.

- Lose confidence. As you keep researching, you'll realize how little you know and risk experiencing more intense feelings of inadequacy, which will prevent you from taking action.
- Come across opposing views and conflicting ideas, which will make the decision-making process much more complicated. Of course, this is not a bad thing per se, and depending on what you are studying, you might need to dig deeper. However, in many cases, you don't need to know all the details to make a decision. The less important the decision is, the less research you probably need to do.

To cultivate deep focus, you must dramatically reduce useless input. Otherwise, you'll suffer from what is often referred to as "information overload" which will usually lead to "analysis paralysis".

1. How to avoid information overload

Information overload is simply the act of consuming more information than you need. Of course, we all consume information we don't necessarily use right away, if ever. However, if you go too far in that direction by consuming too much information too quickly, you'll probably start feeling overwhelmed.

The key is to consume the right amount of information to meet your needs. For instance, a doctorate student will need to consume far more information than an employee asked to write a brief report for their boss.

When you find yourself searching for information, I invite you to do the following:

A. Determine exactly what you're trying to learn or accomplish.

If you don't know why you're consuming information, you'll end up spending too much time looking for data you don't need in the first place. On the other hand, once you know what you need, you'll be able to:

- Search for the information in the right place and under the right format (books, articles, videos, reports, et cetera),
- Identify the people who are likely to have the information you need, and
- Decide exactly the amount of information you'll consume and for how long.

Many people are caught in the trap of learning or researching more than they need to. One reason for this is that it feels good to learn new things. It gives people what is sometimes referred to as "the illusion of competence". As we consume more and more information, we start believing that we are becoming smarter and more competent. However, this is often not true. In most cases, we need to act on what we learn to achieve the results we desire. By doing so, we're able to convert theoretical knowledge into practical wisdom.

Now, let me give you some examples of information overload.

First, let's start with a personal example—book writing. Writing a book can take anywhere from a few weeks to a few years. It all depends on the length of the book and the reason we're writing it. A researcher might need to spend years before they can write a book in their field. On the other hand, an expert who wants to write a short practical guide to offer to potential clients may be able to do so within a few weeks, considering they already have the knowledge and just need to put it into a book.

When I write a book, I keep in mind what I'm trying to accomplish with it. I might first write a simple outline to help determine the information I want to cover. Then, I will do some research as needed. Finally, I will set a specific deadline for the project. By doing so, it will automatically reduce the scope and force me to be smart with the way I spend my time.

On the other hand, if I read book after book for research, I will quickly feel overwhelmed. Encountering too many irrelevant details, I will lose sight of the overall picture and make writing more challenging. Therefore, whenever I start feeling overwhelmed, it's usually a sign of information overload. In which case, I stop and take a step back.

Now, let's say you want to learn a foreign language. If so, you need to define why you want to learn it. Is it to read books in that language? Is it to have a conversation with your friends? Or is it to use it at work?

Based on your needs, you must then adopt your learning strategy. If you want to have a conversation in that language, this is what you should focus on. You don't need to read all the grammar books available. You can simply hire a teacher and find a language exchange partner to meet every week. Then, later on, if you feel the need to fine-tune your skills, you might buy a book on grammar.

The point being, information overload comes from a lack of clarity regarding what you're trying to learn or achieve. Gain clarity on that and plan accordingly. This way, you'll become much more productive.

B. Reverse your learning-to-action ratio.

Most people spend way too much time consuming and not enough time implementing. In short, there is a lot of input, but not much output. To boost your productivity, you must learn to reverse your learning-to-action ratio. That is, you must act more and study less. This alone will make a massive difference in your life. By taking more action you'll:

- Have much more clarity regarding what needs to be done. As a result, you'll be less likely to suffer from information overload and analysis paralysis,
- Learn faster by receiving more feedback,
- Accomplish more, and
- Feel better about yourself for achieving your goals.

I invite you to take a step back and look at your learning vs. action ratio. Of course, how much you need to learn as opposed to taking action will depend on the task at hand. However, you can always take more action. Taking action toward your goals is one of the best cures against information overload.

Tip:

Stop learning for thirty days. If you find yourself taking on too much new information, stop studying anything new for the next thirty days. Don't read any new books. Instead, take as much action as you can, using what you've already learned.

Action step

Using your action guide, write down your weekly activities. Then separate them into two categories: learning and doing. Finally, write down at least one thing you could be doing (or stop doing) to reduce the input (i.e., what you learn), and increase the output (i.e., what you produce) instead.

DAY 7—ELIMINATING FRICTION AND ENERGY WASTE

Clutter is not just the stuff on your floor—it's anything that stands between you and the life you want to be living.

— PETER WALSH, RECORD PRODUCER.

To deepen your focus, you must remove any unnecessary friction and prevent energy waste as best you can. Whatever you're trying to focus on, you'll often experience resistance, especially when that task is truly important. For example, writers sometimes experience writer's block. They may have all the time in the world to write, yet they do anything but write. I've written over twenty books, and I still experience resistance (though I'm much better at overcoming it these days).

Put simply, "eliminating friction" means making undesirable behaviors or activities as difficult as possible to engage in, while making desirable ones as easy as possible to perform.

As for eliminating "energy waste", it means lowering the switching costs between tasks and making the transition from one task to another as smooth and easy as possible.

Let's work on eliminating friction first, shall we?

I. Eliminating friction

What prevents you from focusing on your most important task right now? How much willpower is required to begin working on it? Our brain is energy efficient and doesn't like to make any unnecessary effort. Consequently, to reduce the risk of becoming distracted and procrastinating, you must make the tasks you want to work on, the default choice. That is, they must be easy to get into. Conversely, you want to make unproductive tasks much more difficult to start.

To give you an example, if you put your favorite cake on your desk within easy reach, you'll end up eating it at some point during the day (probably sooner than later). But if you have to leave the house and traipse all the way to the supermarket to buy it, there will be much more friction and you'll be less likely to eat the scrummy delight.

The same thing goes for major tasks you want to focus on. For instance, if you want to write, some ways to reduce friction are:

- Writing first thing in the morning, before doing anything else (eating breakfast or taking a shower),
- Making your file on your computer accessible in one click, or even better, leaving it open so that it's the first thing you see when you wake up your computer, or
- Writing in a distraction-free environment.

These actions will reduce friction significantly and make it much easier for you to actually write.

Now, you also want to make it harder to engage in any other activities that distract you from your main tasks. To do so you could:

- Turn off your Wi-Fi,
- Put your phone on airplane mode, and/or
- Use a timer.

Finally, as we mentioned before, you can implement a daily ritual to put yourself in the right state of mind and condition yourself to write (or do anything else that you want to work on). As I'm writing this, I'm listening to relaxing music using headphones. And before I start writing, I perform a simple morning routine that consists of drinking water and taking some vitamins before sitting at my desk. I sometimes use a timer as well.

The point is, the more you condition your mind through daily routines, the easier it will be to tackle your task. As you build a solid habit of doing your hard work daily, it will become easier and easier. Sure, you'll still "relapse" occasionally, but at least you'll have the tools that will help you return to work whenever you need it.

Now, let's see how you can eliminate energy waste.

2. Eliminating energy waste

Our mind is often looking for ways to avoid hard work. Whenever we perceive a task as challenging, we can experience resistance. We may doubt our ability to complete it effectively, or we may be afraid the pay-off won't be there (e.g., what if my book doesn't sell?). As a result, the more we give our brain room to think, the more it will succeed in convincing us not to do the work. It will tell us things such as:

- We can always do it later.
- Let's just check our emails first.
- We should do more research. I don't feel completely ready, do you?
- I feel like having a coffee, do you?

Sound familiar?

To avoid such issues, you must give less room for your mind to trick you into lethargy. One effective strategy is to plan your day effectively. By knowing what your key priorities are, you are less likely to be distracted. You'll start to notice whenever your mind tries to steer you away from your main work. The transition from task A to task B will also be smoother.

On the other hand, if you fail to write down your goals each day and decide what to do on the spot, you'll often end up performing make-work tasks. You'll tend to travel along the path of least resistance, letting your lazy mind decide what you should be doing. And that's really not the way you design your ideal life.

Therefore, I recommend you dedicate time each day to planning. To do so, simply take a pen and a sheet of paper and write down the few key tasks you must focus on that day. Visualize yourself completing them. Then, commit to doing them. The simple act of writing down your key tasks each morning will do more for your productivity and focus than almost anything else you can ever do.

Action step

Using your action guide, select a task you want to work on today or tomorrow. Then, write down what you can do to remove as much friction as possible. Finally, create a simple routine to help you start work.

Plan your day by writing down on paper three tasks you'd like to complete today. Move from one task to the next deliberately and take notice of whenever your mind tries to distract you.

CONCLUSION

Your ability to focus is one of your superpowers. When you learn to focus more deeply and more consistently, your productivity will explode, and you'll find yourself accomplishing far more than you could ever have imagined.

I hope the exercises in this book have helped you enhance your focus and boost your productivity. I would strongly urge you to revisit them whenever needed. When you notice you're losing focus and becoming overly distracted, give yourself seven days to get back on track by re-reading this book and completing all the exercises.

You won't always be as focused as you'd like to be. And that's okay. But if you can be just a little more focused than most of your peers, you'll notice a major difference over time. So, if you want to attain your bigger goals, you know what you have to do!

Wishing you all the best,

Thibaut Meurisse.

ACTION GUIDE

I. Gain Clarity

Day 1—15 questions to identify what you want

Reflect on yourself and answer these questions. If you're unsure with your answers, that's okay. You can revisit and refine your answers later on.

A. Eliciting your desire

1. What do you really, really want?

2. If you were to wake up tomorrow, completely alone without any family member, friend or colleague to influence your decisions, what would you do differently?

3. If you were to be totally honest with yourself, what would you start doing now? What would you stop doing?

4. If you were guaranteed to succeed in everything you do, where would you want to be in three years?

5. If you could spend your day exactly the way you wanted to, what would you be doing from morning to night? What would your ideal day consist of?

6. If you could focus only on doing one thing for the rest of your life, what would it be?

7. If you understood and truly believed you could achieve absolutely anything you want by sticking to it for long enough, what would you pursue in the next three to five years?

B. Finding your strengths and unique abilities

8. When are you the happiest at work and what are you doing?

9. What do you find so easy to do you genuinely wonder why others struggle to do the same thing?

10. What do people around you say you're great at?

C. Uncovering your passion

11. What did you enjoy doing when you were a kid?

12. Who do you envy and why?

13. If you had all the time and money in the world, what would you do?

14. If you had complete confidence and were already your absolute best self, what would you be doing with your life?

15. How do you want to express yourself to the world?

Day 2—Gaining clarity regarding what you want

Assess your goals

Write down what you really want. Then try to assess if these are love-based or fear-based goals. You can put "L" for the love-based ones, and "F" for the fear-based ones. Feel free to continue on a separate sheet of paper if needed.

Things I want	L/F

Day 3—Gaining clarity regarding what needs to be done

Revise your strategy

Select a major goal you're currently working on or want to focus on. Now, ask yourself, If I keep doing what I've been doing today or this week, will I achieve that goal? If not, what would need to change?

Now, time to come up with a specific strategy by answering the questions below. You can keep revising your strategy over time:

1. Who has achieved a similar goal in the past?

2. Is there a book or course I could purchase to help me achieve that goal?

3. What are the very few things I should focus on to reach that goal?

Day 4—Gaining clarity regarding how it needs to be done

Reduce your learning curve

Two things you need to focus on to reduce the learning curve:

1. Find the right information
2. Get help from people who've already achieved your goals (or similar ones)

1. Find the right information

First, define your learning goals as clearly as possible. To help you do that, answer the questions below:

a. What exactly are you trying to learn or do?

b. Why exactly do you need to learn it or do it? why do you need to tackle this task? How does it fit the big picture?

c. What do you want the final result to look like? Make sure you can articulate in great detail what you want the final result to be like.

2. Get help from people who've already achieved your goals

If you know someone who has achieved your goals in the past, I encourage you to "interview" him or her. You can ask the following questions:

a. What was your learning strategy?

b. If you could choose only one thing, what do you think is the one activity that was the most effective for you?

c. What did you struggle the most with? How did you overcome it?

d. If you were to learn that skill all over again, what would you do differently?

e. If you were in my shoes, how would you go about learning it?

f. Is there anything else I should know?

The answers to these questions should help you significantly create an effective plan.

Remember, to develop deep focus, you must know what to focus on. Asking people who have been there done that is an effective way to do so.

II. Eliminate distractions and obstacles

Day 5—Simplifying

A. Practice ruthless elimination

First, make a list of all the activities you're engaging in in a typical week.

Now, ask yourself the following question: knowing what I know now, would I still engage in this activity? You can also do the same for projects you're working on, products or services you're offering etc.

Implement the blank slate technique.

Imagine you could create your schedule from scratch while having the total freedom to eliminate any activities you like. What would your new minimalistic schedule look like?**Learning to say no**

Now, write down what you could say no to next time and how exactly you'll decline the request.

B. Minimize Distraction

Internal distractions

Write down 2-3 specific things you will do to reduce internal distractions

_____

_____

_____

External distractions

Write down 2-3 specific things you will do to reduce external distractions

_____

_____

_____

Day 6—Reducing useless input

Determine exactly what you're trying to learn or accomplish.

Write down your weekly activities. Then separate them in two categories: learning and doing.

Learning	Doing

Now, write down at least one thing you could be doing (or stop doing) in order to reduce input (i.e. what you learn) and increase output (i.e. what you produce) instead.

_____

Day 7 - Eliminating friction and energy waste

Select a task you want to work on today or tomorrow. Then, write down what you can do to remove friction as much as possible.

Finally, create a simple routine to help you get started on that task.

Plan your day by writing down three tasks you'd like to complete today. Move from one task to the next deliberately and notice whenever your mind is trying to distract you.

Notes:

Notes:

Printed in Great Britain
by Amazon

67597987R00051